Public Libraries Going
GREEN

Kathryn Miller

ALA Public Library Handbook Series

American Library Association
Chicago   2010

Kathryn Miller is assistant vice president of academic resources at Argosy University. Her educational preparation includes a BA in English from the University of Illinois at Urbana, a JD from the University of Akron, an MLS from Kent State University in Ohio, a library media specialist certification from Dominican University in River Forest, Illinois, and an EdD in adult education from National-Louis University, Chicago, where she worked as a library faculty member until 2009. She also engaged in professional development in 2007 at the ACRL/Harvard Leadership Institute for Academic Librarians and has an extensive background in presentation and publication, covering topics ranging from copyright to online learning styles to library weeding projects. Dr. Miller worked in Michigan as a librarian at the Detroit Public Library and the West Bloomfield Public Library and now lives in Orlando, Florida.

Text pages printed on 50-pound Cascades Enviro 100 Print, a recycled, 100% post-consumer-waste stock. Cover printed on 10-point Productolith Points, a mixed-resources, recycled, 10% post-consumer-waste stock.

The paper used in this publication meets the minimum requirements of American National Standard for Information Sciences—Permanence of Paper for Printed Library Materials, ANSI Z39.48-1992. ∞

Library of Congress Cataloging-in-Publication Data
Miller, Kathryn, 1971– .
Public libraries going green / Kathryn Miller.
    p.   cm. — (ALA public library handbook series)
  Includes bibliographical references and index.
  ISBN 978-0-8389-1018-4 (alk. paper)
  1. Library buildings—Environmental aspects—United States. 2. Library buildings—Energy conservation—United States. 3. Libraries and community—United States. 4. Public libraries—United States. 5. Environmental education—United States. I. Title.
  Z679.85.M55 2010
  022'.314—dc22

                                                                                              2009040319

ISBN-13: 978-0-8389-1018-4
Printed in the United States of America
14 13 12 11 10   5 4 3 2 1

CONTENTS

ACKNOWLEDGMENTS

Many, many thank-yous to those who have believed that green is so much more than a color—a way to live, learn, and lead libraries.

Thank you to Stephanie Zvirin, acquisitions editor at ALA Editions, for her guidance. Her belief in this project is greatly appreciated.

Thank you to Gail Bush for her belief and trust in my work and for all of her wonderful contributions to libraries in Illinois.

A tremendous amount of appreciation to Kathy Walsh for her leadership in creating a green library before green libraries were acknowledged or understood. Also, many thanks to the leadership at National-Louis University in Chicago for their progressive ideas on education and library learning, particularly Dr. George Litman and Dr. Carol Melnick. Thanks to the great library staff and faculty at National-Louis, particularly Mark Burnette, Jerry Dachs, Barbara Evans, Larissa Garcia, David Hoogakker, Dr. Carole Kabel, Linda Lotton, Dr. Rob Morrison, Carol Moulden, Don Pawl, Toby Rajput, Marisa Walstrum, and Victoria West-Pawl.

A special thank-you to the many professors who worked with me through the adult education doctoral program at National-Louis University, particularly Dr. Scipio Colin III, Dr. Thomas Heaney, and Dr.

Randee Lawrence. I hope the readers of *Public Libraries Going Green* realize that every person is a learner throughout her life. Knowingly and unknowingly, people continuously learn. This book is a beginning guide on how every person can learn, change their own behavior, and help influence a greener world. To the family of Dr. Elizabeth Peterson, may you know that Dr. P. touched so many people with her kindness and gentle teaching style. She is greatly missed.

Thank you to Dr. Kathy Tooredman, an educational leader and visionary as well as a believer in the value and purpose of the green library. Dr. Tooredman, thank you for the many opportunities you have given me to lead and effect change.

To Timothy, Geoffrey, Clare, and Grace, we have experienced so many changes in life—each change for the better. Always remember to embrace change and understand that you can affect how change happens. Your kindness to others will return kindness to you.

Thank you to my parents, Jim and Tricia Metzinger, for their encouragement in my career. Also, thanks to my husband, Todd Miller, for his undying support, and to his parents, Jesse and Judy Miller, for their help and generosity.

INTRODUCTION

Throughout modern history public libraries have provided "the resources for citizens to become informed about events and thus able to participate in the democratic process with greater knowledge."[1] A public library provides its community with the resources it needs to learn, understand, and grow.

As learners need change, so do public libraries. Change may be reflected in the resources made available to the community, the learning tools provided at the library, or the educational offerings made available at the library. Now, in the twenty-first century, public libraries are challenged with the new role of connecting the public with environmental awareness and education. Public libraries are challenged to go green.

What Does It Mean to "Go Green"?

Our society relies on Earth's resources for food, health, and life. It is the human race's responsibility to protect and preserve Earth's resources. Sustainable living, defined as one's ability to live a life that makes as little negative impact on the environment as possible, is the underlying goal of "going green." Living a life that protects, preserves, and replenishes Earth's resources is a green lifestyle. Public libraries have an important role in green living. As the "gateway to knowledge," a public library can be the community's resource for understanding how to live green, both as an example in being green and as a green education resource.

The need to "go green" is not a new concept but one that has risen in popularity and in media exposure as the concept of global warming has become prevalent in the news and popular media. People are beginning to understand that the decisions they make about how they live their lives directly affect the environment. Global warming is the result of what is known as the greenhouse effect, the trapping of greenhouse gases in the atmosphere. Urban sprawl, car and aircraft emissions, and coal-generated power all contribute to increased temperatures on Earth.[2] The idea of "going green" is to reduce the amount of greenhouse gases we trap. "Going green" is an effort to save our planet by making better choices for its health.

Legislation

Countries have worked together to aid the reduction of greenhouse gases. The 1997 Kyoto Treaty, which outlined the importance of world-wide efforts to help the world's population "go green," is an example. This treaty is an agreement among countries for each country to make individual efforts to reduce its greenhouse emissions. The Kyoto Treaty set a date of 2012 by which developed nations would release fewer greenhouse gases than they did in 1990. The United States and Australia have not ratified the treaty.

In the United States, federal legislators have taken steps to help protect Earth by passing environmental laws. Many of these laws are administered by the U.S. Environmental Protection Agency (EPA). Examples of environmental laws in place that help the United States "go green" are the Clean Water Act; the Clean Air Act; the Safe Drinking Water Act; the Resource Conservation and Recovery Act; the Comprehensive Environmental Response, Compensation, and Liability Act; the Federal Environmental Pesticide Control Act; and the National Environmental Policy Act.

The Clean Water Act, originally passed in 1972, regulates the discharge of pollutants into the nation's surface waters, including lakes, rivers, streams, wetlands, and coastal areas. The EPA administers this act by setting water quality standards and helping state and local governments develop state-specific water pollution control plans.

The Clean Air Act, 42 U.S.C. §85, originally passed in 1970, protects air quality. This legislation sets standards for air quality and specifically limits the types and amounts of pollutants that can be released into the environment. This act is also administered by the EPA.

The Safe Drinking Water Act (SDWA), 42 U.S.C. §300, provides water quality standards that help protect the quality of actual and potential drinking water in the United States. Water quality standards and control are handled by many states, and state standards for drinking water must be at least as stringent as the federal standards.

The Resource Conservation and Recovery Act (RCRA), 42 U.S.C. §6901, provides rules about how solid and hazardous waste can be generated, handled, and disposed of in the United States. This law, originally enacted in 1976, has been amended to stay current as society and its waste products have changed. The EPA administers the RCRA and provides a searchable database of publications, outreach, and other materials that relate to the rules of the RCRA at www.epa.gov/waste/inforesources/online/index.htm.

The Comprehensive Environmental Response, Compensation, and Liability Act (CERCLA), 42 U.S.C. §103, passed in 1980 and amended as the Superfund Amendments and Reauthorization Act (SARA) in 1986, is a federal law that addresses how the cleanup of hazardous waste sites should be handled. This law, commonly referred to as the Superfund, gives the EPA authority to require property owners or operators to clean up hazardous waste sites or, if the responsible party cannot be found, to clean up the site using a special trust fund. The Superfund laws also create retroactive liability for parties who were involved in the hazardous contamination of property.

The Federal Environmental Pesticide Control Act (FEPCA), a 1972 law that updates the 1947 Federal Insecticide, Fungicide, and Rodenticide Act (FIFRA), gives the EPA power to regulate the use and sale of pesticides to "promote human health and preserve the environment."

The National Environmental Policy Act, 42 U.S.C. §4321, originally passed in 1970, requires the federal government to consider the environmental impact of potential projects as part of its decision-making processes. An environmental impact statement must be prepared and reviewed by the EPA before a project may begin. Environmental impact statements are available in an online searchable database at www.epa.gov/compliance/nepa/eisdata.html.

The Mercury Export Ban Act of 2008, which prohibits the export of elemental mercury from the United States, was signed into law on October 14, 2008, as Public Law No. 110-414 and was effective on January 1, 2010.

There have been many proposals for new federal laws that would help protect the environment but have not been passed into law. States and cities, however, have taken a lead on developing and implementing environmental laws. An example of a state law that aims to protect the environment is New York State's Plastic Bag Recycling Law (Assembly Bill A11725/Senate Bill 8643-A). Effective in January 2009, the law requires large retail and chain stores to accept clean plastic bags for recycling.

States have been implementing a variety of laws that direct how electronic products can be disposed of. Many states place the burden of providing a recycling program on the producers of the product. States that have an electronic waste disposal law in place or in process include the following:

Hawaii: Electronic Device Recycling Act
Illinois: Electronic Products Recycling and Reuse Act
Maine: Electronics Waste Recycling Law
Missouri: Manufacturer Responsibility and Consumer Convenience Computer Equipment Collection and Recovery Act
New York: Electronic Equipment Recycling and Reuse Act
Oklahoma: Computer Electronic Recovery Act
Oregon: Oregon E-Cycles
Pennsylvania: Manufacturer Responsibility and Consumer Convenience Computer Equipment Collection and Recovery Act
Rhode Island: Electronic Waste Prevention, Reuse and Recycling Act
Tennessee: Manufacturer Responsibility and Consumer Convenience Information Technology Equipment Collection and Recovery Act
Texas: Manufacturer Responsibility and Consumer Convenience Computer Equipment Collection and Recovery Act
Washington: E-Cycle Washington

Arizona, California, Connecticut, Indiana, Maine, Maryland, Massachusetts, Michigan, Minnesota, New Jersey, North Carolina, South Carolina, Vermont, and West Virginia also have versions of electronic waste disposal laws. To review the laws of each state, visit the Northwest Product Stewardship Council (NWPSC, www.productstewardship.net/index.html)—a coalition of government organizations in Washington and Oregon that operates as an unincorporated association of members.

On a city government level, New York City has many green laws and directives that aim to reduce the amount of waste discarded and to promote waste prevention, recycling, and composting. One of the city's progressive green laws is Local Law 86 of 2005 (effective in January 2007), which requires "most City construction and renovation projects to meet certain standards for green building. Projects that cost over $2,000,000 must achieve a LEED Silver or higher rating. Projects of higher value are subject to more stringent regulations."[3]

Another example of a local environmental law is San Francisco's mandatory composting law, which was passed in 2009. This is a very specific law that requires residents and businesses to sort their waste into three separate color-coded bins for recycling, compost, and waste. Food scraps must be composted and not included in the waste bin. This law includes a steep fine for those who do not properly sort their waste.

As more and more localities pass ordinances or laws that require educated choices, the library can be a leader and teach the community how to understand and comply with the new legislation.

Your public library is a vital component in connecting your citizens with the knowledge and tools they need to "go green"—to change their habits and make the smallest impact possible on Earth's limited resources. This book outlines ways that an existing public library can take steps to be green, teach green, and lead green. Public libraries going green: this is the next chapter in the growth and history of the public library.

Notes

1. K. McCook, *Introduction to Public Librarianship* (New York: Neal-Schuman, 2004), 71.
2. NASA, Safeguarding Our Atmosphere, www.nasa.gov/centers/glenn/about/fs10grc
   .html; Earthjustice, Global Warming, www.earthjustice.org/our_work/issues/
   global-warming/index.html.
3. NYC.gov, NYCWasteLe$$ Agencies and Schools, www.nyc.gov/html/nycwasteless/
   html/at_agencies/laws_directives.shtml.

THE LIBRARY'S GREEN ROLE  1

As our world becomes more environmentally conscious, your public library has the opportunity to become a community example of environmental friendly practices, an environmental leader. An environmental leader is a person or group who acknowledges and accepts the responsibility to set an example as one who bases decisions on how his or her action or choice will affect the environment. A public library can be an environmental leader:

> Leadership is all about personal choices. Leaders strive to be the best they can be, not only for themselves, but for those they serve. Environmentalism is all about personal choices, too. In the face of what seems at times to be almost overwhelming environmental bad news, it is reassuring to know that *each one of us can make a difference*. Each small personal victory adds up to a major impact on our planet's future.[1]

Environmental education is a second green role that your public library can embrace. Environmental education ties into the educational role of the library as a specific type of literacy: environmental literacy. Environmental literacy is "the capacity to perceive and interpret the relative health of environmental systems and take appropriate action to maintain, restore, or improve the health of those systems."[2]

Environmental leadership and education are growth opportunities for the twenty-first-century public library.

Environmental Leadership

Public libraries have traditionally served as vehicles for societal progress within their communities. As President Barack Obama states, "The library has always been a window to a larger world. A place where we've always come to discover big ideas and profound concepts that help move the American story forward."[3] Michael Gorman, past president of the American Library Association, explains: "The printed text allowed us to conquer space, in that many copies were available in many places, and also to conquer time, in that a text printed in, say, the 17th century and held in libraries today is available to us and will be available to future generations."[4] Throughout history, libraries have contributed to the progress of human knowledge. In the twentieth century, public libraries began to expand their role beyond books and materials and into the use and comprehension of Internet technology. Examples include public libraries' development of web pages, database use, and, most recently, the use of blogs, Twitter, Facebook, and other Web 2.0 applications to communicate with their communities. Now, in the twenty-first century, public libraries have the role of teaching environmental awareness through library programming and services. Environmental education is yet another way that the public library can help its community take another step toward societal progress.

The public library also plays the role of leading by example. By making pro-environment decisions and adopting pro-environment practices, the public library leads its community by example.

Change is effected through education and by example. The public library is well positioned to effect environmental change. This book provides a public library with ideas about how it can help its community understand their environment and help them make pro-environment choices. With budgets tight and resources becoming more and more expensive, finding funding for green initiatives is tricky. Ideas about how to bring a green atmosphere to your library without making major budget commitments are included.

Environmental Education

Public libraries now have the opportunity to help create environmentally literate communities. Modern environmental education focuses on environmental literacy, a green parallel to information literacy. According to one definition, "To be information literate, a person must be able to recognize when information is needed and have the ability to locate, evaluate and use effectively the needed information." As "information literacy is the ability to find and use information," environmental literacy is the ability to identify a sustainable choice and make that choice.[5] A 2003 report from the National Science Foundation's Advisory Committee for Environmental Research and Education found that "in the coming decades, the public will more frequently be called upon to understand complex environmental issues, assess risk, evaluate proposed environmental plans and understand how individual decisions affect the environment at local and global scales."[6] This forecast points to the need for environmental literacy.

The National Environmental Education Foundation's 2005 report "Environmental Literacy in America" included specific strategies for improved environmental literacy in this nation.[7] Many of the steps suggested in the plan can be effectively achieved by public libraries:

1. Achieve a base of environmental knowledge in America.
2. Organize delivery of environmental education content.
3. Extend environmental education to professionals.
4. More effectively deploy off-site centers, people, and places.
5. Maximize information technology for environmental education delivery.

Through environmental education, we will be taking steps to create environmentally knowledgeable people—people who are able to translate their environmental knowledge into pro-environment behaviors.

According to the plan, environmentally knowledgeable people are

- 10 percent more likely to save energy in the home
- 50 percent more likely to recycle
- 10 percent more likely to purchase environmentally safe products
- 50 percent more likely to avoid using chemicals in yard care

People who are aware of their environment and recognize the effects personal choices can have on our natural resources are more likely to make environmentally sound decisions. Educating people about the environment is key to changing human attitude and action.

An environmentally literate community is one where environmentally knowledgeable people work together to influence the way their community views and uses the environment. The public library can be a hub to put environmental education into the hands of communities throughout the United States. Your public library can effect change through environmental education, creating environmentally knowledgeable people and an environmentally literate community.

Where to Begin?

How does a public library begin becoming green? A first step in becoming green is to develop an action plan that can serve as a road map for the directions and choices your library makes. Your action plan does not have to be detailed; it can simply be an outline of your library's goals.

An action plan does not have to be cumbersome, and the action plan template shown in figure 1.1 can help jump-start your library's efforts to be green. Begin your action plan with your overall purpose (it can be as simple as "To be green"). Carol A. Brey-Casiano, ALA president in 2004/5, suggests that "one of the most critical elements of the action plan is the

---

FIGURE 1.1
Action Plan Template

Description of Project
To position the library as a leader in environmental action and education.

Project Goals
Become a community leader in environmental education
Become a community example in eco-friendly practice
Establish environmentally friendly practices in library facilities
Initiate a community-wide discussion regarding recycling and energy usage
Increase community awareness of environmentally friendly practices
    through library programming

TASKS	TIMELINE	PERSONS RESPONSIBLE	STATUS
Meet with Board of Trustees to discuss green initiative	January	Library Director, Head of Children's Service, Head of Adult Service	Meeting took place. Action approved by Board.
Establish green committee	January	Library Director	Committee members chosen. Committee met January 20.
Analyze current practices used by the library	February	Green Committee	
Invite environmental expert to library to address staff	March	Green Committee	
Develop plan on waste reduction in the library	March	Green Committee, Library Director	
Develop environmental programs	April	Head of Children's Service, Head of Adult Service, library staff members	
Prepare press release discussing the library's green initiative, actions, and plans for the community	May	Green Committee, Library Director	

overall purpose."[8] This is why you are beginning this project, as well as the goal this project seeks to accomplish.

Once your action plan's purpose has been established, communicating that purpose to your community is essential. Brey-Casiano urges libraries to develop a message that matches their purpose (this can be as simple as "Your Hometown Public Library Is Going Green"). With a concise message, your library can deliver its "going green" purpose and goals to library workers, the community, vendors, and potential community partners. A descriptive message not only communicates your library's going green, but also provides an easy way to share your vision with those who can help shape and cultivate your library's efforts.

Community Partnerships

The local business community can be an active partner in your library's efforts to bring about a greener community. Your action plan can be a good tool to introduce your library's plan to go green to local businesses who may be able to support your efforts through funding, programming, or advertising your programs.

To help facilitate business interest in the greening of your community, your library can establish a green award to recognize local businesses and services that have taken steps to be green. School and Community Assistance for Recycling and Composting Education (SCARCE) of Glen Ellyn, Illinois, has developed an "Earth Flag for Businesses." The Earth Flag program is a model for showing that businesses are a friend of the environment. To earn an Earth Flag, the business, organization, or school needs to follow several steps specifically outlined by the organization. Sample steps that need to be taken to earn the Earth Flag include organizing the initial environmental movement at an office meeting, sponsoring an ongoing recycling program at the office, volunteering at a community event that benefits the environment, and sponsoring a waste- or energy-reduction activity (e.g., collection event, composting). SCARCE spells out specific steps for businesses, schools, and organizations on its website (www.bookrescue.org). The SCARCE Earth Flag is a standard-size flag that can be proudly hung on a standard flagpole, clearly announcing that this business, school, organization, or library is environmentally conscious. The SCARCE flag is also available as an image to display on a website. More than thirty businesses have earned SCARCE's Earth Flag.

This program is an example of how one agency can influence environmental learning and action. Public libraries can study the SCARCE Earth Flag program as an exemplary award-based program in environmental and community awareness that both announces a business or organization's commitment to the environment and gently guides the business community through a series of steps to be green.

Your public library can also be a partner in the implementation of local legislation. Many local government bodies are proposing and passing legislation that will help sustain our resources. Public libraries should identify the environment-related laws that are being passed in their own state, town, and community and be an advocate, as well as a possible trainer, for those new laws. Examples of local legislation include San Francisco's mandatory composting law and New York City's local green building law.

Partnering with community businesses and organizations will help connect your public library to other groups, with the great potential to expand your own user base. Brey-Casiano notes that the local news media is a valuable partner: "We often think of the media as our adversaries, but members of the media can prove to be your biggest supporters. Most reporters and others associated with the news media believe in intellectual freedom, which creates a common ground from which to start."[9] With the help of the local news media, your library can inform your community about your plans to go green. Your local news media can also be excellent vehicles for your community to learn about the green programs and other offerings that will be available at your library.

Notes

1. Environmental Leadership, What Is Environmental Leadership? http://environmentalleadership.com/default.htm.
2. ERIC Development Team, "Environmental Literacy," ERIC/CSMEE Digest (ED351201 1992-11-00). www.eric.ed.gov/ERICDocs/data/ericdocs2sql/content_storage_01/0000019b/80/12/f4/a7.pdf.
3. B. Obama, "Bound to the Word," *American Libraries*, August 2005. www.ala.org/ala/alonline/resources/selectedarticles/obama05.cfm.
4. "The Value of Information for National Development," Keynote speech at Libraries: Networking for National Development conference, Jamaica, November 22, 2007.
5. C. A. Brey-Casiano, "From Literate to Information Literate Communities through Advocacy," in *Current Practices in Public Libraries*, ed. W. Miller and R. M. Pellen (Binghamton, N.Y.: Haworth Information Press, 2006), 182–183.
6. No Child Left Inside, Why Is Environmental Education Important? www.cbf.org/Page.aspx?pid=947.
7. K. Coyle, Environmental Literacy in America (2005), www.neefusa.org/pdf/ELR2005.pdf.
8. Brey-Casiano, "From Literate to Information Literate," 185.
9. Ibid., 188.

THE LIBRARY AS A GREEN PLACE

2

Your public library has the opportunity to be a community example of environmental awareness and conscious green behavior. In this chapter we look at ways a public library can be a green place.

Sustainable Buildings

A green library begins with a sustainable building. A sustainable building is a building that meets the needs of today's users but does not compromise the health and availability of Earth's resources. New construction allows planners to create a building that will coexist with the environment, but simple steps can also be taken to make existing buildings more sustainable, or greener.

The United States Green Building Council has developed Leadership in Energy and Environmental Design (LEED) certification, a standard for measuring building sustainability. A LEED building is viewed as a green facility: "LEED certification provides independent, third-party verification that a building project meets the highest green building and performance measures."[1] Several public libraries have achieved LEED certification, including Darien Public Library in Darien, Connecticut, the Bronx Public Library in New York, and the Hillside Public Library in Multnomah County, Oregon. LEED certification allows these libraries to be examples within their communities of environmental leadership through action.

The New York Public Library system has made a commitment to sustainable buildings as exemplified by its Bronx Library Center, a LEED-certified building. The Bronx Library Center is an actively used building and a central vein of community life in the Bronx borough of New York City. The library features typical library service areas including adult services and children's services. Computer labs with computer instruction and education rooms, including an area dedicated to English classes for speakers of other languages, are also available. This library is a community leader in environmental education.

Environmental education at the Bronx Public Library begins with its building. Library users are able to experience examples of environmentally conscious design choices such as the placement of lights, wide windows that allow natural light to brighten the library, and low-flush toilets in the bathrooms.

Louis La Grippo, the senior construction manager for the New York Public Library, explains that New York City's commitment to environmental awareness begins with the buildings but depends on the attitudes and choices made by the employees and users of the library. Environmental choices are a team effort, and every person on the New York Public Library team has to be educated about how to make the best choices for the environment and how to help users make the best choices as well.

Environmental learning is about support as well as knowledge. New York City has the support of its government to encourage and fund environmentally sustainable buildings, the public library has the support of its employees to help the library make choices that have the least impact on the environment, and the people of New York City have the example of the beautiful, environmentally conscious Bronx Library Center to help them learn about and guide their own environmentally conscious decisions for their own homes and businesses. The plaque announcing the Bronx Library Center's LEED certification is a reminder for every library employee and user that the environment comes first at the New York Public Library.

With categories for both existing buildings and new constructions, LEED has developed a point system with varied values for different green building practices. Various levels of LEED certification based on the number of points (out of a total of sixty-nine) that your building earns. There are five broad credit categories from which to obtain points: Sustainable Sites, Water Efficiency, Energy and Atmosphere, Material and Resources, and Indoor Environmental Quality. To become certified at the base level, a library building needs twenty-six points. Silver certification is available at thirty-three points, gold at thirty-nine points, and platinum at fifty-two points.

LEED provides libraries with checklists and relevant points for green elements. LEED certification considers many environmental factors within a building, including the efficiency of indoor plumbing fixtures and fittings, the water efficiency of landscaping, energy efficiency performance, and pest management.

Investigating LEED certification can be a learning experience in sustainable building practices for any public library. Figure 2.1 is a letter that introduces LEED and the library's goal of obtaining LEED certification. Any public library can use this as a template to begin the LEED conversation with its board of trustees.

The Darien Public Library, another LEED library building, adds one more green element to its environmentally friendly location: preferred parking spots for environmentally friendly vehicles. Hybrid cars and any of the other LEED-certified automobiles are eligible for preferred parking at the Darien Public Library. Each environmentally friendly parking spot is designated with a sign similar to a handicapped parking sign but with an environmental designation (see figure 2.2).

Sustainable Products

Although LEED certification is a goal a library can reach for, public libraries can begin making the library building greener by choosing sustainable products. In this section we review some examples.[2]

Paint

A coat of paint can bring new life to a library's indoor spaces. Choosing the right paint helps bring green to your library.

A paint shade can brighten an indoor space, naturally saving electricity. Light-colored paint reflects the sun's heat and makes the room brighter during the day, reducing the need for artificial light.

FIGURE 2.1
Sample LEED Introductory Letter

Dear Board of Trustees,

Anytown Public Library wants to go green.

As a team, Anytown Public Library is attempting to foster Anytown's commitment to environmental stewardship.

Through water and energy conservation and the use of environmentally smart materials including paint and cleaning supplies, Anytown Public Library is striving to be an example of sustainable leadership in our community.

Anytown Public Library proposes to follow standards set by the U.S. Green Building Council. The guidelines under consideration would apply to all building-related issues at Anytown Public Library. These standards are part of the Leadership in Energy and Environmental Design (LEED) program, which uses a Green Building Rating System to register and certify green buildings. The LEED Green Building Rating System assigns point values to different green building practices and then awards a certain level of certification based on the number of points that a building achieves. There are five broad credit categories, with a total of 69 available points: Sustainable Sites, Water Efficiency, Energy and Atmosphere, Material and Resources, and Indoor Environmental Quality. To become certified at the base level, Anytown Public Library will need 26 points. Additional points may achieve a silver (33 pts), gold (39 pts), or platinum (52 pts) certification. Anytown Public Library wishes to seek LEED certification and join the many public libraries in the United States that are recognizing and making a commitment to sustainable practices.

Anytown resident Helen Conley comments, "It's great to see the public library taking the lead to bring green buildings and green consciousness to Anytown. The public library's efforts will make us all better in the long run."

With the Board's support, Anytown will begin preparing an action plan for LEED certification.

Thank you,
Innovative Library Director

Typically, indoor paint is either latex, in which water is a major ingredient, or oil-based, which contains a solvent that does not mix with water. Latex is safer to use, does not require a special product for cleanup, and can be recycled. Oil-based paint can contribute to air pollution and have harmful effects on the environment if improperly disposed of.

When selecting paint, librarians should work with their maintenance staff to read carefully the labels of paint considered for use inside the building. The American Coatings Association offers a glossary of terms commonly found on paint labels (www.paint.org/industry/glossary.cfm). Consulting this glossary can help you determine whether your paint is made from natural ingredients or contains chemicals that may be hazardous to the environment.

Green Seal (www.greenseal.org), a nonprofit organization that aims to validate environmental excellence, provides detailed standards for environmental safety on more than forty categories. As explained on its website, Green Seal provides "science-based environmental certification standards" for products that are environmentally friendly. Products that are certified by Green Seal go through an approval process that looks at the materials life cycle: "We utilize a life-cycle approach, which means we evaluate a product or service beginning with material extraction, continuing with manufacturing and use, and ending with recycling and disposal." Only products that meet the Green Seal environmental standards are awarded the Green Seal. A Green Seal on a product certifies that the product has gone through scientific testing and that it has little impact on the environment.

**FIGURE 2.2
Preferred Parking Supports the Environment**

Used with permission of the Darien (Connecticut) Public Library.

To help consumers identify safer paints, Green Seal has created a series of criteria to evaluate the environmental impact of paints and coatings. Librarians can use Green Seal's website to identify paints that are certified by Green Seal as environmentally friendly products.

Not all paint manufacturers have gone through the Green Seal certification process. Librarians can understand what is inside a can of paint by reviewing its Materials Safety Data Sheets (MSDS), many of which are available online. An MSDS provides information about a product, including the manufacturer's contact information, hazardous ingredients of the product, physical and chemical characteristics of the product, fire and explosion hazard information, health hazard data, and recommendations on safe handling and use.[3] Several databases offer MSDS access, some of which offer free trials or access to free initial MSDS:

> MSDSonline, www.msdsonline.com
> MSDS Solutions, www.msds.com
> MSDSXchange, www.actiocms.com/msdsxchange/english/
>   index.cfm
> MSDS Hazard Communication Library, www.msdshazcom.com

If you need help understanding more about a particular ingredient listed on a paint can label or MSDS, visit the University of Akron's searchable Chemical Database at http://ull.chemistry.uakron.edu/erd/.

It can be difficult to weed through and understand all of this technical information. Key factors in choosing a paint are its toxicity level and its level of volatile organic compounds (lower is better).

Determining the correct amount of paint needed for your project is important as well. For one-coat coverage, one gallon can cover approximately 400–450 square feet. Paint professionals recommend using the full can of paint and not saving any left over. If one coat does not use up all your paint, add coats on sections of the wall until the can is empty and ready for recycling.

Some painters end up with extra latex paint and bring their leftover paint to local household hazardous waste collections. Many communities send leftover paint to paint manufacturers for recycling. Recycled latex paint is made primarily with leftover but unused latex and is typically available for purchase less expensively than "new" paint. Use of recycled paint helps the environment and provides the library with a high-quality and economical paint choice for its new look.

Cleaning Agents

Environmentally friendly cleaning agents also have the Green Seal certification mark available to ensure that the product meets Green Seal's evaluations on the product's life cycle and its impact on the environment. Use of environmentally friendly cleaners is a green initiative your library can pursue. Not all materials clearly label a product safe or not so safe.

Recognizing how to read the labels on cleaning agents can help a public library make the best environmental choices. The terms "nontoxic," "natural," "environmentally friendly," and "biodegradable" do not have standardized meanings. Without standard definitions, a product can claim to be any of these terms, but such claims do not represent that the product has any particular environmental benefit. The following, from GreenerChoices .org, explains the language found on the labels of many cleaning agents:

> *Danger* refers to products that are corrosive, extremely flammable, highly toxic, or poisonous. Commercial toilet-bowl, oven, and drain cleaners often bear this label.
>
> *Caution* or *Warning* are catchall terms for many other hazards, so scan for specifics, such as "Vapor harmful," "Causes burns," or "May be fatal or cause blindness if swallowed."
>
> *Irritants* refer to substances that cause injury or inflammation on contact.
>
> *Corrosives* refer to chemicals that destroy tissue.

It is also vital to know what ingredients are potentially harmful. Some potentially harmful ingredients identified by GreenerChoices.org and sometimes found in cleaners include these:

> Nonylphenol ethoxylates (NPEs). When they're released into the environment, these chemicals can break down into toxic substances that can act as hormone disrupters, potentially threatening the reproductive capacity of fish, birds, and mammals. NPEs are found in many cleaning products, especially detergents, stain removers, citrus cleaners, and disinfectants.
>
> Butyl cellosolve (also known as butyl glycol, ethylene glycol, monobutyl). Poisonous when swallowed and a lung tissue irritant. Found in glass cleaners and all-purpose cleaners.
>
> Hydrochloric acid. Can severely burn skin, irritate eyes and respiratory tract. Found in toilet bowl cleaners.
>
> Naphtha. Can cause headaches, nausea, and central-nervous-system symptoms with overexposure. Found in furniture and floor polish and glass cleaners.

Libraries can choose to work with the most environmentally friendly products by asking for Green Seal products. The GS-8 standard is the Green Seal environmental standard for general purpose, bathroom, glass, and carpet cleaners used for household purposes. Many GS-8 products are used in library maintenance and cleaning. Green Seal certified products that may be useful as cleaning agents in libraries include those listed in table 2.1.

Libraries could also consider making their own cleaning agents out of environmentally friendly materials. Of course, this would be additional work for the library staff responsible for building maintenance, but it would make a strong environmental leadership statement to your community. Sample homemade cleaning solutions from GreenerChoices.org that could be used by a public library include these:

- Baking soda and lemon juice: To remove odors, combine 1 teaspoon baking soda and 1 teaspoon lemon juice with 2 cups hot water in a spray bottle.
- Baking soda: To eliminate carpet odors, sprinkle baking soda on the carpet, let it stand for 20 minutes, and vacuum.
- Borax and vinegar: For a general sanitizer, combine 2 teaspoons borax with 4 tablespoons vinegar and 4 cups hot water in a spray bottle.

Additional recipes for cleaning solutions can be found at the Recipe Goldmine (www.recipegoldmine.com/house/house.html) and Eco-Cycle (www.ecocycle.org/hazwaste/recipes.cfm).

Cleaning Tools

A public library can also choose to use environmentally friendly cleaning tools.

Brooms. Every library has a collection of brooms. When buying your next broom, look at how it was made. Broom bristles can be made from recycled soda bottles. Broom poles can be made from recycled aluminum. Also, when you need another broom, do you have to purchase an entirely new broom, or can you simply replace the bristles? An example of an environmentally sustainable broom is the Eclipse Broom by Casabella (www.casabella.com). When you are shopping for brooms that are better

TABLE 2.1
Green Seal Certified Cleaning Agents

MANUFACTURER	PRODUCT NAME
Ace Hardware	Ace Peroxide Cleaner@ Ace Peroxide Cleaner Concentrate
Berkley Packaging Company	Glass Cleaner All Purpose Cleaner Bathroom Cleaner
Ipax Cleanogel, Inc.	Green4Kleen
Nexgen Chemistries	Responsibly Clean Rug and Carpet Cleaner Responsibly Clean Bath and More Cleaner Responsibly Clean Heavy Duty Cleaner
Office Depot	Office Depot green All Purpose Cleaner (OD802) Office Depot green Glass Cleaner (OD803) Office Depot green Bathroom Cleaner (OD804)
OurHouse an EnvirOx Company	Heavy Duty Cleaner (H1051) Shiny Surface Cleaner (H1052) Carpet and Upholstery Cleaner (H1054)
Simple Green	Simple Green Naturals Multi-Surface Care Simple Green Naturals Bathroom Cleaner Simple Green Naturals Glass & Surface Care Simple Green Naturals Floor Care Simple Green Naturals Dilutable Concentrated Cleaner
Simoniz USA	Green Scene All Purpose Cleaner Deck and Fence Wash Green Scene All Purpose Cleaner House and Siding Wash Green Scene All Purpose Cleaner Wash and Wax Green Scene All Purpose Cleaner and Degreaser
Source Direct Holdings, Inc.	Simply WoW Cleaner/Degreaser Simply WoW Cleaner/Spot Remover
Worx Environmental Products	All Natural Hand Cleaner

Source: Green Seal, www.greenseal.org/findaproduct/hhcleaners.cfm (retrieved May 3, 2009).

for our environment, do not be influenced by brooms that are green in color; green-colored brooms are not necessarily environmentally friendly.

Mops. When you are shopping for a new mop, consider a microfiber mob. Microfiber mops clean without the need for chemicals. Microfibers, in this commercial context, are fibers that measure less than 1.0 denier in diameter. The smaller the diameter of the fiber, the more effective it is for cleaning surfaces. According to Mission Mop (www.mission mop.org), a manufacturer of microfiber mops, microfiber yarns cling "to the smallest particles like a magnet," thus picking up dirt without the need for chemicals. "Each fiber is split during manufacturing making the tiny fibers very absorbent so the mop holds sufficient water for cleaning yet doesn't drip. The mop pad leaves the floor only slightly damp allowing it to dry quickly after cleaning." Thus you save water by not needing to refill a water bucket constantly, and since microfiber mops have washable heads you can wash them in the laundry to keep them in good working order. Microfiber mops are available directly from Mission Mop and from Starfiber (www.starfibers.com).

Vacuum cleaners. When purchasing vacuum cleaners, be careful to choose one that will serve the library for a long time. Vacuum cleaners that are bought for a cheap price and quickly disposed of only add to landfills, thereby hurting the environment. When you are purchasing a new vacuum cleaner, consider how much electricity the product uses. Electricity in vacuum cleaners is measured by amperage (amps)—the flow rate of electrical current that is available. According to Ecollo (www.ecollo.com), a website devoted to educating everyday eco-conscious people, a green vacuum cleaner is one that has an eight-amp motor or can at least operate in a power-saving mode. Other environmentally friendly features to look for in vacuum cleaners include filters that are washable and reusable and, if the vacuum has a dust bag, it should not be made from paper that has been plasticized.

Lighting

A public library can also choose to use environmentally friendly lighting both inside and outside. Geothermal power, solar energy, and wind power are all forms of green energy. Powering a library with energy from the earth is a great goal for a public library, but short of that you can take practical steps to cut back on the energy source already in use by the library.

The U.S. Department of Energy estimates that 30 percent of energy use is dedicated to lighting. Compact fluorescent light (CFL) bulbs are energy-efficient bulbs that are more expensive but use 75 percent less electricity and last five to seven times longer than traditional incandescent lightbulbs. With the savings CFLs can bring to the library, it makes financial sense to purchase the more expensive, environmentally friendly CFL bulbs. Some CFL users claim that the light is different, and that is true. The color of CFL bulbs changes as the bulb heats up. Color ranges for CFL bulbs are listed on the bulb's package. CFL light that is most similar to a standard incandescent lightbulb is in the warm white color range between 2,650 and 2,800 degrees Kelvin.

> Correlated color temperature:
> 2,650–3,200 K: warm white (yellowish white)
> 3,200–4,000 K: neutral
> Above 4,000 K: cool (bluish white or daylight)

Motion-activated light switches can also help a library save energy. A motion-activated light switch uses sensors to dim a lightbulb by 50 percent and can save up to 35 percent of the energy used by a fully bright bulb. Sensors currently have a range of 150 or 180 degrees of motion sensitivity and 15-, 30-, and 60-minute and 24-hour times. Motion-activated light switches are available in many styles and range from switches that need to be wired into your lighting system to ones that simply plug into an existing electric socket.

Many libraries are victims of "vampire power"—the standby power used by chargers for cell phones, iPods, and other electronic equipment. Standby power is typically 10–15 watts per device; a half dozen devices on standby power use as much power as a 60-watt lightbulb burning.[4] Some of this waste can be saved with the use of digital timers. A library can set a timer to turn on for a couple of hours prior to the library's opening, fully charge battery-based electronic tools, and then turn off. Use of a digital timer could save a library twenty-three hours of vampire power use each day.

Outside lighting includes landscape lighting and other accent lighting, and these can be powered by the sun. The benefits of solar landscape lighting include energy efficiency as well as an immediate reduction in energy bills. With solar landscape lighting, the source of energy is the sun. The solar panels that convert the sun into energy are composed of photocells that charge the solar battery. Each fixture consists of a rechargeable battery that lasts for eight to ten hours of continuous use. LED (light-emitting diode) lamps, which have a lower energy consumption and longer lifetime than traditional lightbulbs, can be used for illumination in solar landscape lighting, which allows each fixture to last for a long time. Solar lights also have built-in sensors that turn the lamps on and off automatically, allowing for maximum use and minimum staffing commitment from the public library.[5]

Water

Efficient use of water helps your community conserve water resources and also helps save the library money. A library can take some simple steps to reduce its water usage.

Waterless urinals, which save an average of 45,000 gallons of water per year per urinal, can be installed. According to the *GreenTech Bulletin* of the Kansas State Department of Architectural Engineering and Construction Science, for example, one Texas elementary school retrofitted its restrooms with ten waterless urinals and realized a 15–20 percent reduction in water consumption.[6]

Low-flush toilets also contribute to lower water usage in the library restroom. Low-flush toilets look like regular toilets, but they use about half the water, typically 1.6 gallons per flush instead of 3.5 gallons per flush. Most low-flush toilets hold around 13 quarts of water, but only 6 quarts are flushed through at a time. Some low-flush toilets offer the option of a half-flush for liquid waste.[7]

Water conservation extends to sensor-operated faucets, in which the water flow stops when the user removes his hands from below the water spout. Sensors are also available for the toilet flush valve and work to prevent a user from flushing multiple times. Sensors in a library restroom also contribute to improved hygiene.

Even if your library cannot take the steps to install low-flush toilets at this time, every library should consider purchasing bathroom tissue (also known as toilet paper) that is made from recycled paper. According to the Natural Resources Defense Council, "If every household in the United States replaced just one roll of virgin fiber toilet paper (500 sheets) with

100% recycled ones, we could save 423,900 trees."[8] Public libraries can make a contribution to this effort by purchasing bathroom tissue made from recycled paper, making it available for library users, and letting users know that they are using a recycled product. Greenpeace recommends that you consider following three criteria when purchasing recycled tissue:

1. The tissue should be made from 100 percent overall recycled content.
2. The product should be made with a minimum of 50 percent post-consumer recycled content.
3. The product should not be bleached with chlorine or toxic chlorine compounds.[9]

Recycled bathroom tissue is available from a variety of companies, including Green Forest (www.greenforest-products.com), Seventh Generation (www.seventhgeneration.com), and Small Steps by Marcal (www.marcalpaper.com).

Take the next step and let your users know you are using recycled bathroom tissue. If they like it in the library, they may decide to purchase the recycled product for their own home. Inside each bathroom stall, post a discreet sign such as the one shown in figure 2.3.

Transportation

How do people get to your library? Walking and biking are green ways to travel, and your library can encourage users to walk or bike to the library by ensuring that safe routes are in place. Your library can prepare walking and biking route maps so users understand the best ways to get to the library without a vehicle. These route maps can also work as encouragement for people to come to the library on foot or on a bicycle. Work with your city or town officials to identify stop signs, streetlights, and pedestrian walkways that need to be in place for safe walking and bicycling access to your library. Your library could work with your city to develop a personalized bike and walking map service that maps out the best way users can bike or walk from their home to the library. Bicycle parking, typically in the form of bike racks, encourages people to bring their bicycles to the library and store them. The following national

FIGURE 2.3
Publicize Recycled Products

In our effort to be sensitive to the environment, **this bathroom uses recycled bathroom tissue.**

groups offer ideas on how your library can help encourage users to visit your library by walking or cycling:

> Alliance for Biking and Walking,
>> www.peoplepoweredmovement.org/site/
> America Bikes, www.americabikes.org
> League of American Bicyclists, www.bikeleague.org
> National Center for Bicycling and Walking, www.bikewalk.org
> U.S. Federal Highway Administration, Safe Routes to School,
>> http://safety.fhwa.dot.gov/saferoutes/

Is your library accessible by public transportation? Public transportation is green transportation because it directly cuts down on the number of vehicles on the road. Contact your location transportation office for route maps, time schedules, and more information on the types of public transportation available and accessible to your library. Making bus and train route maps and schedules available in your library encourages library users to come to the library by public transportation. Also, personalized bus and train route planning can help encourage users to come to your library on buses or trains.

Notes

1. U.S. Green Building Council, www.usgbc.org.
2. Except as otherwise noted, the following product information is drawn from Consumer Reports, GreenerChoices.org: Products for a Better Planet, http://greenerchoices.org.
3. Penn State University Environmental Health and Safety, What Does an MSDS Tell You? www.ehs.psu.edu/help/info_sheets/msds_tips.pdf.
4. C. Long, Energy Cost of PCs on Standby (2006), http://news.bbc.co.uk/1/hi/programmes/click_online/4929594.stm.
5. J. Goodman, Solar-Powered Landscape Lighting, http://ezinearticles.com/?Solar-Powered-Landscape-Lighting,-the-Alternative-Energy-Option&id=970526.
6. Kansas State Department of Architectural Engineering and Construction Science, GreenBuild Tech Bulletin (2004), http://files.bnpmedia.com/EDC/Protected/Files/PDF/2005_01-GBTB-WaterlessUrinal.pdf.
7. How to Choose a Low Flush Toilet, www.ehow.com/how_4493176_choose-low-flush-toilet.html?ref=fuel&utm_source=yahoo&utm_medium=ssp&utm_campaign=yssp_art.
8. Natural Resource Defense Council, A Shopper's Guide to Home Tissue Products, www.nrdc.org/land/forests/gtissue.asp.
9. D. Kessler, How to Shop Smart, Save Forests and Send a Message, www.treehugger.com/files/2009/02/greenpeace_how_to_shop_smart.php.

GREEN SERVICES AT YOUR LIBRARY

3

Natural resources are required for many library business functions, ranging from materials purchasing to the delivery of an item to a user. In this chapter we look at choices that can make your library's everyday activities greener.

Materials Arriving at Your Library

Collection development—the practice of building, managing, and maintaining library resources—is an opportunity for public libraries to be leaders in environmental awareness. The behind-the-scenes delivery and processing of library materials has the potential to be cluttered with packaging and other protective materials that end up in the rubbish pile. Packing materials including boxes, envelopes, DVD sleeves, mailing cushions, and shipping labels are available as compostable, sustainable, biodegradable, and recyclable materials. Asking a vendor if they use environmental packaging sends a message that your library is concerned about the environment; demanding environmental packaging tells a vendor that you are a leader in the environmental movement and that the vendor needs to meet your needs.

Eco-friendly packaging and shipping options are available from book and library material vendors. Knowing and understanding four essential eco-friendly packaging terms can help you understand how these products help your library in its efforts to go green:[1]

Compostable: Solid products such as food scraps and plant material such as leaves and dirt that can be broken down by the action of naturally occurring microorganisms such as bacteria, fungi, and algae.

Biodegradable: Products that can be broken down into harmless by-products by the action of organisms.

Recyclable: Products that can be made into new products to use again with minimal alteration.

Sustainable: Products created to have the least impact on the environment. Sustainability considers the production, processing, and distribution of a product. A sustainable product is one that is created using a smaller ecological footprint.

It is important for your library to ask for materials that are friendly to the environment. Asking for and putting an importance on the use of environmental shipping and packaging materials will make a difference to your library's carbon footprint.

Interlibrary Loan

Interlibrary loan is a green library service because it matches users with their information needs and avoids duplication and overbuying in library collections. This collaborative sharing of resources, however, often requires packaging materials for transport from library to library. When interlibrary loan takes place through the mail, a library can use environmentally friendly packaging and shipping materials. As a general practice, however, libraries should first look to see if requested materials are available from a nearby library. Often libraries in close proximity can share materials through an interlibrary loan process that delivers materials in bins, avoiding the need for excessive shipping materials.

The paperwork involved in interlibrary loan can be extensive. Computerized software programs are available to manage your interlibrary loan functions and reduce the paperwork involved in the process. ILLiad Resource Sharing Management Software (see www.oclc.org/illiad/) is an example of a software program that "lets your staff manage all of your library's borrowing, lending and document delivery through a single, Windows-based interface. And it lets users serve themselves, via the Web." With ILLiad, your users are able to request needed materials through an Internet-connected computer. Users create an account, submit the citations of the items they need, and can check the account for the status of the requested materials. For articles or chapters of books, requested materials can even be delivered to their online ILLiad account. Paper is saved in the requesting, processing, and delivering of each interlibrary loan document. Problems with handwritten requests are eliminated with the computer-entered loan requests, and your library is able to gather statistical information about interlibrary loan requests that can be used for collection development and funding purposes.

Paper

Your public library probably uses a significant amount of paper with its copy machines and computer printers. Purchasing and using recycled paper at your public library directly help conserve natural resources by not requiring additional trees to be cut down and used as paper. Conservatree (www.conservatree.com) offers libraries and other consumers an online guide to specific brands of paper, environmental information about the paper, and national and regional locations where paper can be purchased. It also offers an online guide on how to read the label on a ream of paper.[2] This guide helps consumers understand the information on the ream wrapper. Conservatree encourages consumers to "look for the percentage of postconsumer content, this is the single most important thing to look for," when purchasing paper. Your public library can access Conservatree's label-reading information and link it to your website—an easy way for your library to communicate good environmental choices to your community.

Post-consumer content is material that has already served its intended use, has been discarded for disposal, and is now being used again. Such material must be distinguished from pre-consumer content, also found in recycled products. Pre-consumer content is scraps or leftovers from the manufacturing or processing of paper or other goods that are being recycled to become a new product.[3]

Both pre- and post-consumer fiber is seen in recycled paper, but post-consumer fiber is paper that is truly recycled—used by one person, placed in a recycling bin, and reused to create an additional resource that can be used by someone else. The use of recycled paper in your public library not only saves trees but demonstrates to your community that recycled paper is good-quality paper that can be purchased easily.

Stanford University encourages its community to reduce the amount of paper used: "In addition to purchasing recycled paper, it is easy to reduce your paper use by using double sided copies and printing drafts of documents on the blank side of paper that has already been printed on once."[4] Public libraries can follow Stanford's example and can also encourage users to send materials found on the Internet to an e-mail account to be accessed later. Teaching your library users how to cut or copy and paste text from one window into another helps them understand how websites and other information can be entered and saved in a personal e-mail account. Another easy step is to make your library's computers accessible to pen (flash) drives, so that users can save information they find or create at the library and not necessarily have to print out everything they encounter online.

A library also purchases paper in the form of books, magazines, newspapers, and other print materials. It is essential that your library recognize the value of materials printed on recycled paper and communicate with your vendors that your library values and requests products that use recycled paper. In a 2005 *USA Today* article, Carol Memmott restates Greenpeace's mandate for book publishers: "Greenpeace wants book paper to be 100% recycled or, at least, a combination of recycled paper and wood pulp not harvested from old-growth or endangered forests." Memmott continues, explaining that when Greenpeace asked its e-mail list to request that Scholastic, the U.S. publisher of the Harry Potter series, conform to Greenpeace's standard mandate, Scholastic heard from more than 12,500 individuals.[5] Such communication from end users sends a very important message to the publisher: people want to read books on recycled paper. Your library can have the same impact by insisting that materials be printed on recycled paper.

When you are requesting and working with recycled paper, it is important that you understand the related terms:[6]

> *Recycled paper:* Simply, paper that contains recycled fiber. This is a broad term that can apply to paper that contains as little as 10 percent post-consumer fiber to as much as 100 percent post-consumer recycled.
>
> *Virgin fiber paper:* Paper that is manufactured without the use of any recycled or alternative fibers.
>
> *Chlorine-free process:* Paper recycling process in which the recycled content is bleached without chlorine or chlorine derivatives. Chlorine-bleached paper can form toxic compounds, known as dioxin and furans, that can accumulate within humans and other animals and may cause serious health problems.

These terms set the stage for additional, very important terms:[7]

> *AFF, ancient forest friendly:* AFF paper is totally chlorine free (TCF) or processed chlorine free (PCF) and contains only the following fibers: post-consumer recycled fiber (PCR); de-inked recycled fiber, agricultural residue, or tree-free virgin fiber; or Forest Stewardship Council (FSC) certified virgin fiber.
>
> *FSC certified papers:* The Forest Stewardship Council (FSC) is a nonprofit organization that has developed standards that ensure forestry is practiced in an environmentally responsible, socially beneficial, and economically viable way. A FSC logo on paper indicates that the company producing the paper has followed socially and environmentally responsible practices in the marketplace.
>
> *Alternative or tree-free paper:* Paper created from nontree resources including cotton rags, recovered denim scraps, agricultural fibers, hemp, flax, or kenaf (a member of the hibiscus family).

In addition to the type of paper used, also be aware of the value of a publisher using soy or other vegetable-based inks. Soy ink contains varying amounts of soybean oil, which often replaces petroleum oil, making the ink lower in volatile organic compounds (VOCs) that react with other atmospheric pollutants to form smog. It is easier to recycle paper printed with soy-based inks than petroleum-based inks, for the inks are removed more effectively from the paper, resulting in less hazardous waste and reduced treatment costs.[8]

Know these paper terms, understand what you are buying, and communicate to your vendors that your library is interested in materials published on recycled paper. Your library can take these steps and easily claim a role as an environmental leader.

Digital Material Choices

Public libraries must also consider how they provide materials to their users. With the availability of electronic books, digital articles, and streaming media, does your library need to purchase materials for a physical shelf? Consider offering your users materials in a digital format.

Electronic collections are environmentally friendly and extend a library's services, but will your community use these digital information resources? The best way to anticipate how your users will accept digital information products is to understand how they use the library. You can do a survey to learn what your users currently use at your library. Figure 3.1 is an example of such a survey.

Digital information resources include electronic books, audiobooks, electronic magazines, music and video, Web 2.0 tools, and various websites. These online products can save physical space as well as processing time and shipping and shelving costs in your library. Also, the availability of Internet-accessible information products increases your number of users by freeing the resources from a single physical location. With online information products, your Internet-enabled community members can access library resources from wherever they choose. Though it is great to have users visit the library, Internet-based content enables users to find information at home or at work; they can avoid having to drive their car to the library to find an answer to a question, thus saving gas and reducing vehicular carbon emissions.

FIGURE 3.1
Sample Web Survey

My Public Library User Website Survey

My Public Library seeks your feedback on library collection so that we may better understand and meet your needs. Thank you for taking the time to help us better understand our community.

Do you use the My Public Library website?

Yes | No

What services do you use at My Public Library website?

Book catalog	Yes	No
Full-text books	Yes	No
Full-text magazines	Yes	No
Reference services	Yes	No
Website links	Yes	No
"My library account"	Yes	No

Where do you access My Public Library website? Circle all that apply:

Home | Work | School | Library

Which library services have you used in the past six months? Circle all that apply:

Electronic books | Print books | Large print books

Electronic magazines | Print magazines | Electronic newspapers

Print newspapers | Video DVDs | Music DVDs

Online reference service | In-person reference service

Interlibrary loan | Storytime | Public computer | Copy machine | Fax

What service would you like to see added to the My Public Library website?

_____

_____

Electronic Books

Electronic books are available in a variety of formats including plain text files (.txt), hypertext markup files (.htm), portable document files (.pdf), and Amazon Kindle (.azw). The most prominent electronic book vendors require the user to download the book to a computer, cell phone, PDA, or e-book reading device. Electronic books have become easier to use, and more titles are available each year. Not all library users, however, have accepted the concept of the electronic book for their reading. The library must balance its purchase of electronic books according to its community's reading and research needs.

Although electronic books are environmentally friendly, they typically cost 30–50 percent more than print books. Still, by buying one electronic book a library can provide many users with sometimes simultaneous access to the book and reduce its need for workers to check the book into and out of the library and reshelve it.

For a public library to collect electronic books, it must first establish several policies. For one, the library needs to choose the electronic format(s) for the books. Once the format is set, it must establish the type of user access. Does the library need to supply the reading device, and if so how will it do this? Is the reading device lendable or for in-library use only? And before making a commitment to any electronic book format, it is important that a library always ask what happens if this book format becomes obsolete; will we be able to read this book using a different format?

Many electronic books are available for a library to access through a license. Electronic book collections now available for library license include NetLibrary, Ebrary, Credo Reference books, Gale Virtual Reference Library, and Overdrive. Books purchased in an electronic format also have end-user licenses attached to them. It is essential that the library understand and comply with the terms of the license. Specific license items to look for include the following:

> *Access:* How is the licensed material accessed by library users? Is this form of access acceptable to your library?
>
> *Users:* How does the license identify users? A public library should try to have wording that allows all of its registered library users to use the licensed material. In this way, the library can make the policy decisions about who has access to its licensed materials.

Compliance: Carefully read licenses to understand your library's compliance commitment to the licensed material. Does the license obligate your library to identify users who should not be using the licensed materials? It is very hard to control persons who do not have a connection with your library, and your library should avoid agreeing to such language in a license agreement.

Public libraries should also be aware of new technology formats for reading books. Examples include Amazon's Kindle, the Sony Ebook reader, and Apple's iPad. These devices allow readers to purchase and read their selected books on a device dedicated to reading books in a digital format. These readers are another green reading avenue that public libraries should carefully watch as the technology and access to electronic books advances and improves.

Audiobooks

An audiobook is a spoken recording of a book's text. Audiobooks can be made available through the library's website, and patrons can download and play them on their personal computer or portable device such as an iPod or MP3 player. LibriVox (http://librivox.org) and Free Classic Audio Books (http://freeclassicaudiobooks.com) offer free audio versions of books that are in the public domain. These audiobook services are examples of how an online service can help the environment by making content available without the library needing to make a space or disposal commitment for the materials.

Electronic Magazines

Many of the issues associated with electronic books are also seen with electronic magazines. Electronic magazine licenses can get tricky, and a library must be sure to understand what it is purchasing. Some licensing issues may include how the publisher handles yearly access to the electronic magazine: does the license provide access to the previous twelve months of the magazine or allow access only to issues of the magazine that have been published thus far this calendar year? It is important for the library to avoid disappointed patrons who expect the magazine to be available for the current year and then find only January through the current month. Licensing terms are something the library should understand before purchasing an electronic-only subscription to a database.

Another issue with electronic magazines in relation to print magazines is the library staff time involved in collecting and managing electronic magazines. Managing electronic magazine subscriptions is an involved process that requires constant updating and attention to detail. Compliance with the licenses must be managed throughout the license period. Although there are services that help librarians make and maintain electronic magazine subscriptions, the time a librarian must devote to making electronic magazines a successful, searchable, and accurate part of the collection is significant.

Libraries must also carefully consider embargos on electronic magazine content, particularly when dealing with an aggregated database. An embargo is a delay placed on the online availability of published material by request of the publisher or author. Magazine or journal embargos can be for a single issue or for as long as six months, depending on the agreement between the publisher and provider of the electronic media where the article will be available. Often, library users want the most current issue of a magazine, and if that magazine has a six-month embargo on it, the electronic version may not be an acceptable substitute for the print magazine.

As with electronic books, the method of access for electronic magazines must also be considered. Many electronic magazines have user names and password access, which a library may or may not want to work with. Proxy server access to the electronic magazine is another way that journal publishers allow libraries to provide access to the journal online. A proxy server is a server that evaluates the login credentials of persons requesting a website; if the person's credentials are valid the proxy server passes the requester through as an authenticated user who can then use the requested materials or service without an additional password.

Proxy access allows users to identify themselves as patrons of your public library and then have access to your licensed electronic materials. Proxy access is a great additional service to library users; clear instructions on how to use the proxy as well as simple processes for users to identify themselves as a member of your public library are essential.

Music and Video

Music CDs and DVDs and video DVDs are popular collections for public libraries, and online versions of these products are available for libraries to license.

The Music Online search tool (www.alexanderstreet.com/products/muso.htm) offers public libraries over 200,000 tracks of streaming music. The music is divided into separate collections that your public library can choose and license for your community. This service offers a public library the opportunity to have a robust music collection without the space and material commitment of housing CDs and DVDs in the library—another example of a library using the Internet to make environmentally friendly decisions while expanding its offerings.

Companies including Discovery Education and United Streaming offer libraries collections of videos that they can purchase and have streamed to their library patrons. These are excellent opportunities for the public library to provide educational films to its patrons with the least environmental impact. Many public libraries also house major motion picture DVDs for their patrons. This is often a popular service at the library but, at this time, not a service that can easily be made downloadable. This is a service area that will probably change, becoming digitally enabled and more environmentally sustainable in the next several years.

In discussions of video content in libraries, Web 2.0 technology is an important topic. Web 2.0, the social Internet, is creating opportunities for libraries to produce their own video content and make that content available to the community. Original video content can be shared on YouTube (www.youtube.com) and TeacherTube (www.teachertube.com).

Here are a few examples of public libraries reaching their public through digital media posted on the Web:

> Columbus, Nebraska's "Discover a New World at Columbus Public Library" YouTube video at www.youtube.com/watch?v=s-oBHCsFbkk. This video features a pop-up book that combines digital still images and live footage in three-dimensional space, encouraging viewers to discover a new world at the Columbus Public Library.

The Allen County Public Library in Fort Wayne, Indiana,
produced an informational tour of the library's Genealogy
Center and posted the video on YouTube at www.youtube
.com/watch?v=tcqDqc0SXgo&feature=related.

The Cincinnati Public Library posted a video on YouTube
providing its community with a sneak preview of the
fun activities planned for its 2009 children's summer
reading program, Creature Feature: www.youtube.com/
watch?v=D_zD4uKVjBM.

Your library can also take advantage of video clips available on the Web.
A great site to visit and use is GardenFork, which features Real World
Green Videos. Real World Green offers practical tips on environmental
issues through weekly online video productions, which are also available
as an iTunes subscription. The videos are created by Eric Rochow, who
also hosts GardenFork, a web video show about cooking, gardening,
and "other fun stuff."

One of Real World Green's videos is "Visiting Your Public Library
Makes You Green." This web-based video can help your library advance
its goals of becoming green. This and other green ideas and videos are
available online at www.gardenfork.tv/real-world-green/.

Videos can also be produced and shared on the library's own website. An example of producing original content and making it available
in a video library is the Public Health Streaming Video Library of King
County, Washington (www.kingcounty.gov/healthservices/health/videos
.aspx). Public libraries have the ability to be information producers as
well as providers. Producing information and placing it in a location that
people can access is another good way the library can contribute to its
community.

Websites

Public libraries can expand their collections by providing users with access
to websites that support the mission of the library. Selecting content-
based websites that are created and updated by reputable organizations
is a way for libraries to provide more informational resources to their
communities without making the commitment of maintaining those

resources. Examples of content-based websites that will expand a library collection include these:

- The Gold Rush exhibit at the Virtual Museum of the City of San Francisco, www.sfmuseum.org.
- The U.S. Supreme Court's recent opinions, www.supremecourtus.gov.
- Thousands of lesson plans for K–12 teachers, http://teachers .net/lessons/. Many lesson plans on Teachers.net are relevant to libraries and library programming. Lesson 3271, "Purification of Recycled Plastics," is an activity where participants work on teams to figure out a way to purify recycled plastic materials. This lesson could be a fun activity for a young adult librarian to lead.

When offering web-based content to library users, the library should have a website selection system in place, and all websites should be evaluated by designated library staff before they are recommended to the public. A library's website evaluation system is library specific and must consider that library's community and resource needs. A simple website evaluation system reviews at least five elements:[9]

1. Accuracy of the information on the web page. Can this information be verified elsewhere?
2. Authority of the web page. Is the author, along with contact information, listed on the website?
3. The domain of the web page. Is the domain from a .edu, .gov, .org, or .net provider? Does the library want to link to .com sites?
4. Date of publication. Is the information current and is the web page updated regularly?
5. Ability to view the information without fees, excessive pop-ups, or other limitations to accessing the information.

Libraries have traditionally shared selected website choices with their communities through handouts and pathfinders. Delicious and LibGuides are two new online tools that can streamline the recommendation and organization of website selections as well as reduce the need for additional paper use in the library.

Delicious (http://delicious.com) is a free social bookmarking service that allows users to tag, save, manage, and share web pages from a centralized source. Through Delicious, users are able to create a personal set of bookmarks that are kept on the Delicious website, from which they can access them using any Internet-accessible computer. A public library can create a Delicious account for the library or for particular departments. The Delicious account access information can be shared with the library staff who can select websites. A library Delicious account could be advertised on the library web page, along with instructions on how library users could create their own Delicious account (again, it's free). The library can then send library Delicious users bookmarks to web-based resources that the library recommends. Delicious can provide your users with access to library-selected materials as well as contribute to an online community environment with your library users. A public library's presence on a service like Delicious also may make nonlibrary users in your community take a new look at what is offered at their local library.

LibGuides (www.springshare.com/libguides/) is a content management and knowledge sharing service where a public library can enter website recommendations, add YouTube and other videos, and, generally, provide users with an organized way to access web resources. LibGuides help libraries direct their users to Internet information the library has identified as reliable. Here's how the producer puts it:

> Sure, your patrons can use Google, Wikipedia, and online databases to find information. But you, the librarian, are the key to *successful* research. Nobody knows research better! You're the information superhero, the knowledge professional, the info sage. With LibGuides you help patrons find stuff they need and show them information they didn't even know existed. Patrons can even ask you questions in real time, while doing research thru LibGuides.

The LibGuides service must be purchased by the library, but it is an environmentally conscious way for a public library to expand its offerings to its community greatly and an easy tool for a team of library website selectors to share their resource findings with library users.

Information Access: OPACs and MARC Records

Libraries are collections of information. Public library users need to be able to identify and locate specific information within the library. In an effort to help people find what they need, libraries organize their information through catalog systems, call numbers, genres, and material types. Information that is in the library but cannot be found by patrons is equivalent to information lost. Public libraries are making a green statement by having an online public access catalog, or OPAC—a computerized library system that allows a user to enter keywords, author names, and other additional terms to locate items that may match their information need. By having an OPAC a library is able to provide users with searchable access to the library's holdings without the need for paper records to direct users to the information they are seeking. Several different companies sell OPAC systems, and libraries often refer to the OPAC by the vendor's name. The OPAC, essentially, is the traditional library catalog available in a computerized format. OPACs contribute to the greening of the library by using the computer rather than paper to organize and communicate what information is available within, and where it is shelved. An OPAC also provides a library with circulation capabilities, further eliminating the need for paper. Many OPACs now are able to record library user e-mail, allowing the library to communicate directly with patrons, for instance to tell a patron that materials are due or fines owed. This is a paper saver as well as a postage saver.

Most OPACs operate on the basis of MARC (machine readable cataloging) records. MARC records have been a key element in allowing a library's organization to go from paper based to computer based. The information that is added to a MARC record is what users are able to search to locate information within the library. A MARC record is a template consisting of fields and subfields where information on what is contained in a book or other item can be added. Common fields used in MARC records include 100 (Author), 245 (Title), 260 (Publishing information), 300 (Physical description), and 650 (Subject heading). In addition to these, the 500 fields are used to add relevant notes to the catalog record. Each numeric field also has indicators and subfields that are used to specify the use of an entry in the field. For example, a 245 field has two indicators. The first tells the OPAC whether or not the title should be an entry that someone can search under. The second indicator tells the OPAC how many digits it should skip before indexing. Subfields also help identify elements of the field. In our 245 field, for example, subfield a shows the main part of the title, subfield b shows other title information (such as a subtitle), and subfield c shows who is responsible for the title (such as an author). In the example below, the 245 field is used to tell the OPAC to index the title and skip four digits before indexing. It also gives the main part of the title, the subtitle, and the author.

> 245 14 #a The making of modern Holland :
> #b a short history / #c by A.J. Barnouw.

Using the same title, here are other fields that would be used for that book in MARC cataloging:

> 100 10 #a Barnouw, Adriaan Jacob #d 1877-1968.
> 260 #a New York : #b W.W. Norton & Co. #c c1944.
> 300 #a 224 p. : #b map ; #c 21 cm.
> 651 0 #a Netherlands #x History.

Libraries can use the notes field to include information about whether a book is published on recycled paper. MARC field 590 is reserved for local definition and use. This field can be used by a public library to indicate the type of paper used in the book. The key to using the local notes field is to have a consistent entry method for paper types; this helps organize the types of book paper in your collection. With the 590 entry, both indicators are left blank:

> 590 #a Printed on recycled paper.

As local notes, information within the 590 field is used for only that library's copy, and this information is searchable and appears on the catalog record.

David Hoogakker, lead cataloger at National-Louis University in Chicago, advises that public libraries are large consumers of books and have strong purchasing power. This power can be used to help influence the paper publishers use when printing a book. Public libraries can organize the types of paper that are in their books by recording that information in a MARC record. This makes a statement that reflects the libraries' commitment to purchase books made of environmentally sustainable materials and also gives a strong message to the publishers that the type of paper used in book printing is important. In addition to recycled paper, a library can request that books be published with tree-free paper. Tree-free papers contain alternative fibers such as hemp, cotton, and agricultural by-products. Tree-free paper is not necessarily preferable in all cases, but in general it presents a viable alternative. A 590 tag that indicates a book printed on tree free paper would appear as follows:

590 #a Printed on tree-free paper.

MARC tags can also be used to guide users to the electronic books in a collection. The key to collecting electronic books is access; users must know that the books are available in the library. Access and location of the electronic book can be established through the MARC record, thus informing users of the availability of an electronic book through the library's OPAC:

MARC field 020 is the authority record for the International Standard Book Number (ISBN) and allows for the words "electronic book" to be displayed after the ISBN number.

MARC field 245 subfield h allows for the book medium to be included in the record. Here "[electronic resource]" can be indicated.

MARC field 856 provides information about electronic resources. Using the 856 tag can expand your library's collection by providing your users with access to items that are not physically within or necessarily owned by your library. Also, subfield z within the 856 field can be used to state access information for electronic resources (e.g., log in using library card number). With 856 tags, libraries are able to guide their users to high-quality content and not make the commitment of buying that content.

856 tags can be created in an individual library. Web-based resources that are cataloged as part of a public library's collection should be items useful to the users of that library. Also, consistency in how a public library codes the web-based resource is essential. The 856 tag first indicator indicates the access method; the indicator options are 0, e-mail; 1, FTP; and 4, HTTP. The second 856 indicator is the relationship of the electronic resource to the full record: blank is no relationship; 0, resource; 1, version of the resource; and 2, related resource. 856 tags also have twenty-nine subfields that aid organization of the web resource into your

library's own collection. Here's an example of the 856 field from the Library of Congress:

856 40 #u http://lcweb2.loc.gov/ammem/gmdhtml/
gmdhome.html.

Deselection and Disposal of Library Materials

Weeding is an essential part of public library service. What is weeded and what happens to those materials after they are removed from the collection depend on the library's policy on weeding.

Public libraries should have collection development policies in place that explain why and how weeding takes place. Weeding policy statements are typically part of a library's collection development policy. Common weeding language indicates when a collection should be weeded, how the weeding should be done, and what should be done with the materials that are discarded. Many weeding policies do not, however, include language on what to do after material is removed from the collection. This is an issue that should be addressed in every collection development policy. Failure to address what happens to materials once they are deselected may result in those materials being sent directly to a local landfill.

When considering whether materials should be weeded from your collection, public libraries should consider the five As:

Age
Accuracy of information
Appearance
Access or Circulation statistics
Audience

Also, librarians should consider MUSTIE, a formula for determining when an item should be weeded. MUSTIE asks if the material is

Misleading—out of date, inaccurate
Ugly—damaged, worn, taped, ugly bindings
Superseded—by a newer edition
Trivial—does not fit in with the library users' needs
Irrelevant—is not of interest to the local patrons
Elsewhere—is not as good as something available elsewhere

If any of these MUSTIE elements are met, the material is a candidate for removal from the collection. An excellent free manual for weeding modern libraries is available at the Texas State Library and Archives Commission website (www.tsl.state.tx.us/ld/pubs/crew/).

Avoid sending weeded books and other materials discarded from a library collection to a landfill. Instead, make sure your public library identifies and pursues these three Rs: recycle, reuse, or re-create. Public libraries sometimes find that they have materials that have been donated to them but are not going to be included in their collection. These books, as well, should be recycled, reused, or re-created.

Recycle

To recycle is to allow a material to be used again. Recycling is the process of transforming materials that would otherwise become waste into usable resources. According to EPA, recycling brings these benefits:

> Recycling reduces the need for landfilling.
> Recycling prevents pollution caused by the manufacturing of products from virgin materials.
> Recycling saves energy.
> Recycling decreases emissions of greenhouse gases that contribute to global climate change.
> Recycling conserves natural resources such as timber, water, and minerals.
> Recycling helps sustain the environment for future generations.[10]

A book cart offering is a good way to recycle discarded books. Book cart offerings are simple. Create clear signage that explains how interested persons may acquire the books on the cart. "Free Books" or "$1 per book. Donation will be collected at the circulation desk" clearly indicate the library's intention of recycling the books to library users.

When a library begins a strong weeding campaign, it could announce its book cart recycling efforts through its newsletter website, Twitter, or blog. A library could also let the local newspaper know about the availability of new books on the book cart. Remember, the more people who come to your library, the more books you will be able to recycle easily through a book cart, and the more exposure your programs and other offerings will receive.

For those books that are not recycled within your own library, local recycling centers and events can be utilized to recycle books. Updated information on local recycling events for books can be found at Earth 911 (http://earth911.com). You can also search for local recycling centers by zip code at www.recyclingcenters.org.

Reuse

If your weeded books are in good condition, several companies sell books that you no longer want in your collection.

Book Prospector (www.bookprospector.com) is a used-book company that purchases books from individuals and libraries and then resells them. Your library enters the ISBN of a book into the Book Prospector online search engine, which immediately generates a price quote if the company is willing to purchase that book. If you are satisfied with the price quote, all you have to do is click on the "Sell Item" button and send in your book(s), and Book Prospector will send your library a check. Book Prospector even provides prepaid USPS shipping labels. With Book Prospector, libraries can use the "Account Manager" tab to keep track of their earnings from their sold weeded books.

Better World Books (www.betterworldbooks.com) has a similar service. Libraries are able to type in the ISBN of a book and get a price quote. With Better World Books, libraries are paid through PayPal, and for every book that Better World Books sells, it makes a donation to one of its five literacy partners: Invisible Children, Books for Africa, Room to Read, Worldfund, or the National Center for Family Literacy. Your library can choose which literacy partner will benefit from your sale of books to Better World Books.

Friends Book Sale (http://friendsbooksale.com) is a free service that accepts a library's saleable weeded and donated materials and sells them on various Internet sites including Amazon, Half.com, Abe Books, and Biblio. All the library has to do is sign up for Friends Book Sale, and the company will send free boxes and prepaid UPS shipping labels to the library. Friends Book Sale sells the books and gives your library a minimum of 30 percent of the sales proceeds. At its website, Friends Book Sale assures that books it does not sell will be donated or recycled:

Books that do not meet our selling criteria, or are not sold within a reasonable period of time (normally 1 year) are either donated to the St. Vincent de Paul Society in Atlanta, Georgia or are appropriately recycled. No book that we receive will ever find its way into a landfill.

B-Logistics (www.blogistics.com) operates like Friends Book Sale and sells weeded and donated books through the online marketplace. According to its website,

> The B-Logistics online sales program can supplement or replace your traditional community book sales. Because so many books will never find a buyer in your local marketplace, the B-Logistics program helps you expand the reach of your existing bookstore and Friends sales by putting your materials in front of hundreds of millions of shoppers outside your local community.

B-Logistics prepays shipment of the library's chosen books to the company's Denver distribution facility, and the company takes care of the rest. B-Logistics manages all the pricing, selling, customer service, and shipping of your library's materials, and your library gets a sales report and check for your portion of the proceeds each month.

If your library is willing to sell books directly to potential customers, book sales and eBay are options. Many public libraries have Friends groups that sponsor used library book sales. A Friends group book sale is a good way to involve your community in the generation of new revenue for the library.

Public libraries can also consider donating their good-condition weeded and donated books to nonprofit organizations:

Hands Across the Water (www.surplusbooksforcharity.org) collects books and sends them to schools and libraries that need them. According to the charity's website, the company offers a solution to two problems: the domestic problem of excess books going into landfills, and the global problem of not enough books in needy areas. Currently, drop-off locations are located in Massachusetts, Connecticut, Rhode Island, Missouri, Washington, and Georgia, and the charity is looking for avenues to expand into other states.

Reach Out and Read (ROR, www.reachoutandread.com) is a program that works to

> make early literacy a standard part of pediatric primary care. Following the ROR model, pediatricians, family physicians and nurses advise parents that reading aloud is the most important thing they can do to help their children love books and to start school ready to learn.

ROR uses the donated books to distribute to participating ROR clinics throughout the United States. ROR is very clear on the types of books it accepts:

1. Used books must be gently used (covers and pages intact, clean and readable).
2. Hardcover picture books with brightly colored pictures and interesting stories are ideal.
3. ROR's focus is on children between the ages of 6 months and 5 years, although books for older children may be accepted, depending on individual program needs.
4. Books about sensitive issues like divorce, abuse, or death cannot be accepted. If included, they will be discarded.

ROR does not have a book pickup service, so a public library must work with the organization to arrange drop-off or delivery of the discarded and donated library books to ROR.

Books for Soldiers (www.booksforsoldiers.com) is an online service that matches soldiers' wants for reading materials with potential donors. This nonprofit organization maintains a website where soldiers can record their book requests and potential donors can register, join forums, and send their used paperback books to the soldiers. This is a website that combines need with Web 2.0 technologies. Working with this organization could be a good community-building project for your public library as well as a good way to distribute weeded and donated paperback books rather than send them to the local landfill.

Another way to handle books you do not need in your library collection is to distribute them. BookCrossing (www.bookcrossing.com) is one avenue where your library can distribute books. This site tracks donated books left in public places such as train stations or park benches. BookCrossing is a community of book readers who are seeking a challenge to find books and claim books in various locations throughout the world. According to BookCrossing's website, this online community

> is earth-friendly, and gives you a way to share your books, clear your shelves, and conserve precious resources at the same time. Through our own unique method of recycling reads, BookCrossers give life to books. A book registered on BookCrossing is ready for adventure.

To recycle books with BookCrossing, each book needs to be registered in the BookCrossing system and assigned a unique BookCrossing ID. This process is time consuming but free. To enter a recycled book into the BookCrossing system, you supply the book's ISBN and title. Once the book is registered and receives its own BookCrossing ID, BookCrossing suggests that the ID plus something like the following be added inside the book:

> Hello Kind Reader,
> Just a quick note that I've registered this book at BookCrossing .com, so that I can keep up on where it goes, who reads it, and what they thought of it. Please visit www.BookCrossing.com/ (BookCrossingIDnumber) to make a quick journal entry, then pass the book along to someone else who will appreciate it. We can all track this book's journey and the lives it touches forever more! Thank You!

Of course, your library could create a template with this information and simply print out a label with the information and the unique BookCrossing ID.

With the BookCrossing ID in the book, your library can release the book "into the wild," where other people will find it. When someone finds the book, they can go to the BookCrossing website, enter the BookCrossing ID, and register that the book has been claimed. Your public library can watch as books are claimed by one person and then redistributed through BookCrossing, creating a map of where your weeded and donated books have traveled throughout the world. This can be a fun activity for a teen library group to plan, organize, and run using weeded library materials.

Public libraries can also seek persons or groups willing to take the books that are not needed in the collection by posting the information about the books on Craig's List (www.craigslist.org). Craig's List is a collection of classified ads, many of which list items that are free, from more than 570 localities in the United States. Your library might post a notice in the For Sale: Free classified section that it has books available for pickup. It is important that you state what you are giving away and your library's terms for pickup.

Freecycle (www.freecycle.org) is another classifieds-based site, but on Freecycle everything is free. As explained on its website, Freecycle is

> a grassroots and entirely nonprofit movement of people who are giving (& getting) stuff for free in their own towns. It's all about reuse and keeping good stuff out of landfills. Each local group is moderated by a local volunteer. Membership is free. To sign up, find your community by entering it into the search box above or by clicking on "Browse Groups" above the search box. Have fun!

Re-create: Altered Book Art

Books that are no longer needed as part of the library collection can be used as a base for craft projects sponsored by the library. Books can be turned into unique sculptures, pages can be used as framable art, and book spines can be combined to create a statement. This "altered book art" is creativity at its finest. As explained by the International Society of Altered Book Artists (ISABA, www.alteredbookartists.com), "It is any book, old or new, that has been recycled by creative means into a work of art. They can be . . . rebound, painted, cut, burned, folded, added to, collaged in, gold-leafed, rubber stamped, drilled or otherwise adorned . . . and yes! It is legal!" For ideas on altered book projects, visit the ISABA website. Think fun, and run with the project. Can that book be made into a purse? Figures 3.2 and 3.3 are a few examples of projects you might try, and figure 3.4 shows some final products.

Sponsoring altered book art projects is another way to use books weeded from your collection to bring your community into your library.

FIGURE 3.2
The Altered Art Book Safe Project

A book safe is a book with a hidden compartment inside. The hidden compartment can be a great place to hide treasures, extra sets of keys, or even a few extra dollars. With the book safe, this book looks just like others on the shelf—only it has a secret inside.

Materials

one 2-inch or wider hardcover book	pencil	glue and glue gun
	craft knife	scrap cardboard
ruler	scrap fabric	

Instructions

1. Using the ruler and the closed book, measure and mark on the closed book pages a spot at least once inch from the front cover of the book.

2. Open the book to the marked spot and with a pencil create a pattern that will become the hidden compartment within your book safe. The pattern should be at least two inches from the book's sides. Rectangular compartments are the easiest to work with.

3. Use the craft knife to cut out the pattern drawn in step two. Depending on your craft knife, you will probably only be able to cut about ten pages at a time, always removing the paper cutouts prior to cutting the next level.

4. When you get to the last twenty pages of the book, insert the scrap cardboard so that the back cover of the book is not harmed.

5. The scrap fabric will be the liner of your hidden compartment. Cut your scrap pieces of fabric to be the same size as your cutout. The cutout area forms the hidden compartment of the project.

6. Working from the inside of the hidden compartment or cutout, use the glue gun to apply enough glue to the sides of the cutout book pages. The glue here should hold the cutout pages in place. Note: do not use glue on the outside of the book; glue should be used within the cutout area only.

7. Let the glue dry and line the inside of your hidden compartment with scrap fabric.

8. With glue, attach the pages of the hidden compartment to the back cover of the book.

9. Again, let the glue dry.

10. Your book safe is ready. The first sections of the book should be easy to turn and the back sections of the book are immobile, your book safe.

Source: L. Baird and the editors of Yankee Magazine. Don't Throw It Out: Recycle, Renew, and Reuse to Make Things Last. New York: Yankee Publishing Company, 2007.

FIGURE 3.3
Literary Scrapbook Altered Book Art Project

Have families bring in scrapbooking materials—pictures, fabric, stickers, cutouts, tickets, and other mementos. Library staff should identify and have a collection of discarded books that the families can use for their literary scrapbook. If possible, a library-created sample scrapbook should be available for families to see and get ideas. Literary scrapbooks can be only one page that is decorated and then displayed in an open position. Literary scrapbooks can also be a full book, with the discarded book cover decorated as well as several inside pages. Depending on the theme of your literary scrapbook or literary scrapbook event, children's or adult books could be used for this project.

Materials

discarded books	glue gun and glue
scissors	family-supplied mementos

Instructions

1. Have examples of discarded book scrapbooks available.
2. Create an environment where families can get messy with glue, cuttings, and other creative materials. Be sure to set a time frame (e.g., Literary Scrapbook Night goes from 7 to 8 p.m.).
3. Supply families with discarded books.
4. Have a library staff member on hand to help families create their scrapbooks.

If families agree, literary scrapbooks could be featured in your library's display cases.

Recycling Beyond Books

With the overall goal being less waste sent to the landfill, public libraries have the responsibility of disposing of unneeded materials in ways most friendly to the environment. In addition to library books, other materials commonly used in a public library can be recycled, including paper, aluminum, and plastic.

Paper

Paper recycling is recovering scrap paper and remaking it into a new product. Recycling paper is an important step in helping the environment. According to the Paper Industry Association Council (www .paperrecycles.org), more than 80 percent of U.S. paper mills use recovered paper to make new products. A public library's efforts to separate paper from other trash directly support the creation of new products while keeping it out of landfills and incinerators.

To begin recycling paper, a library should work with its maintenance people and local trash removal agencies to develop a paper recycling plan. According to Paper Recycles, many trash haulers offer in-house expertise to help you set up, maintain, or improve your recycling program. More and more companies are making recycling services—including monitoring, measuring, and reporting—part of their waste-hauling contract negotiations.

With a recycling program established, the library must understand which kinds of paper can be recycled and which cannot. Typical items that can be recycled include the following:

> clean white paper
> boxes holding dry food or other dry materials
> newspapers
> magazines
> brown paper bags
> envelopes
> letters
> advertisements
> paper used for artwork

Aluminum

Aluminum beverage cans may not be allowed in the library, but having a collection site outside the library can help people entering the library recycle their cans. According to Green Networld (www.green-networld .com), aluminum cans are collected, remelted, rolled, manufactured, and placed on a store shelf in as little as ninety days from when the used

FIGURE 3.4A
Altered Book Art

A season
in the life
of a family
is something
that never slips away
when you mark it
moment by moment
by love
that etches its way
indelibly
in time.

mark time?

Used with permission of Pam Yee, a Michigan-based artist and active
member of the International Society of Altered Book Artists.

FIGURE 3.4B
Altered Book Art

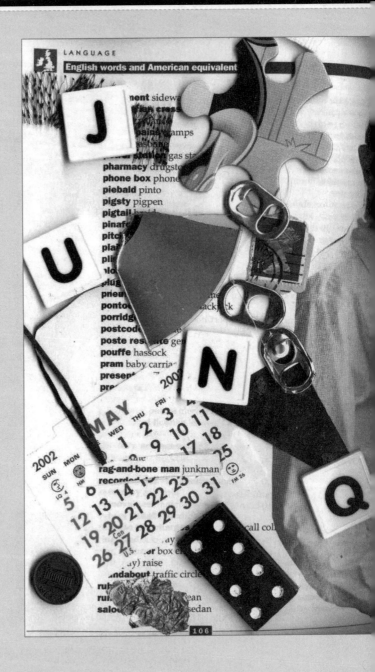

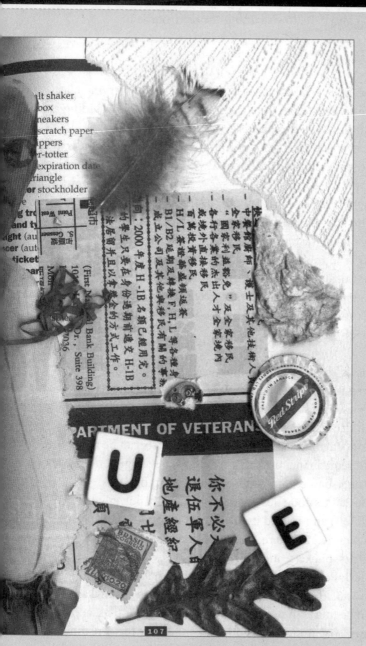

Used with permission of Pam Yee, a Michigan-based artist and active member of the International Society of Altered Book Artists.

can was put in a recycling bin. Recycling aluminum cans is an excellent way libraries can contribute to sustaining the environment.

Plastics

A public library can also recycle plastics. Patrons may be carrying plastic water or juice bottles when they enter the library, and providing a place for these bottles to be recycled is environmentally friendly.

Plastic recycling affects a range of products, from drink containers to shopping bags to pipes. Plastic is almost always the product of petroleum, a nonrenewable resource. This makes recycling plastic even more important. To better understand which plastics are recyclable and to obtain appropriate recycling receptacles, your library should work with your community's local trash removal agency.

A library may also look to the resin identification coding system established by the Society of the Plastics Industry (SPI, www.ides.com) to determine which plastic goods the library may recycle.[11] The SPI code, a triangle of arrows surrounding a number, is often found at the bottom of a plastic product. This number indicates the plastic content, as follows:

> SPI Code 1: These plastics are made with polyethylene terephthalate, or PET. "PET is clear, tough, and has good gas and moisture barrier properties. Commonly used in soft drink bottles and many injection molded consumer product containers." SPI Code 1 products can be recycled and remade into anything from new beverage containers to fiber-based items such as clothing or tote bags.
>
> SPI Code 2: This code designates high-density polyethylene (HDPE) and is used in juice and water bottles. HDPE can be recycled to re-create new plastic products including bottles, buckets, and flowerpots.
>
> SPI Code 3: Polyvinyl chloride (PVC) materials have an SPI Code 3. This plastic product is also known as vinyl and can be found in bottles as well as pipes, floor tiles, and carpet backing. Recycled PVC can reenter the consumer-use chain as a garden hose, decking, and even packaging materials.

SPI Code 4: SPI Code 4 may be found in plastic lids, bottles, and wire. This is low-density polyethylene (LDPE) and can be reused as envelopes and manufactured lumber.

SPI Code 5: Libraries will probably not see SPI Code 5 products often. These are polypropylene (PP) and are often found in automotive products. PP products are recycled to create items including bicycle racks and rakes.

SPI Code 6: Found on protective packaging and food containers, trays, and bottles, SPI Code 6 represents polystyrene (PS), a versatile plastic that can be rigid or foamed. Recycled PS products are reused to make new egg cartons, foam packaging, and even new foam plates, cups, and utensils.

SPI Code 7: SPI Code 7 stands for everything else: "Other. Use of this code indicates that the package in question is made with a resin other than the six listed above, or is made of more than one resin listed above, and used in a multi-layer combination." Recycling products coded SPI Code 7 results in new bottles and other commonly used plastic materials.

E-waste

E-waste is electronic waste. This is a broad term for all electronics, such as mobile phones, television sets, and computers, that are discarded. Electronic equipment that is sent to a landfill is potentially very dangerous. According to GreenerChoices.org:

Electronic equipment contains toxic materials:

Computer and television monitors with cathode ray tubes (CRTs) contain four to eight pounds of lead on average. The EPA has identified electronic products as the largest single source of lead in municipal solid waste.

Printed circuit boards in computers, music players, and other electronic gear contain toxic metals such as chromium, nickel, and zinc.

Batteries may contain nickel and cadmium.

Relays, switches, and liquid crystal displays (LCDs) may contain mercury.

Plastics used in many electronic products also contain flame retardants that are toxic and persist in the environment.[12]

Many states are working to develop laws that require producers of electronic equipment to take back equipment that is no longer needed or is out of date and recycle it appropriately. Until those laws are in place, several state and local governments have electronic equipment recycling programs. In your city, look for a household hazardous waste facility or hazardous waste community collection event. You can find these locations and events by entering your zip code in the Consumer Electronics Association's My Green Electronics widget (www.mygreenelectronics.org). Your zip code will direct your library to the proper places to bring electronic waste. Your library can help make your community aware of city and state resources for properly disposing of computers, televisions, VCRs, fax machines, CD players, and stereos as technology changes.

To help library patrons determine which other materials can be recycled, Earth 911 (http://earth911.com) offers a Local Recycling Widget. A public library can put the widget right on its web home page. There, users can directly search for recycling information by material type and zip code. The library can even change the widget's text to give recycling ideas to the library's web page users.

Buying Recycled Materials

A recycling library also needs to make a commitment to purchase recycled materials when possible. Purchasing recycled materials is an important step in the recycling process, and it can also translate into an opportunity for the library. Consider a library bag program. Your library can purchase bags that can be resold to library users as carry-all bags for their library materials; this is also a great organizational system for users to keep all their library materials in one place. Your library can go fancy or plain with the bags available for sale. Examples of bag fund-raisers include these:

Ecosilk Bags. These bags, made from parachute silk, can be silk-screened with your library's logo. They come in fun, vibrant colors and are soft enough for library users to

tuck an unused bag into their purse. Ecosilk Bags come
from Australia but are available as a fund-raising product
through www.bagladiesofseattle.com.

Bags on the Run. This company offers several bag styles at
www.bagsontherun.com, including "Going Green"
bags—cute, generic bags that have an Earth-friendly
message—as well as blank bags and bags imprinted with
your library logo.

Bags on the Run and Ecosilk and are two examples of companies a
library can partner with to offer its users a reusable resource. With a bit of
encouragement, your library bag purchasers may also use your library
eco-bags at the grocery store and avoid accepting plastic bags, or just
around town to advertise your library.

Other items your library can purchase in a recycled form are paper,
pencils, and printer cartridges.

Purchasing recycled paper seems to be a straightforward step in going
green. But it is important to understand the types of recycled paper available for purchase. As we discussed earlier, recycled paper can be made
from pre-consumer materials or post-consumer fiber. Pre-consumer
materials are leftovers (waste) from the creation of another product;
this is material that has not been used by a consumer. Post-consumer
materials are products that have been used by a consumer and recycled,
such as office waste paper, junk mail and magazines, undeliverable mail
at the Postal Service's dead-letter office, and used shipping packaging.
When you are identifying which recycled paper to purchase, consider
specifying post-consumer recycled paper, which directly supports community recycling projects. If a recycled paper product is not specified
as either pre- or post-consumer, it is most likely being recycled with
pre-consumer products. Although pre-consumer recycling still helps
reuse materials, post-consumer recycling directly reuses materials that
have been used for another purpose and recycled.

Purchasing recycled paper for your library should not be more expensive than purchasing virgin paper, and recycled paper is available in
every grade that you could need for your library. To let your community know that you are using recycled paper and to let them experience
the quality of recycled paper, your library can label materials that are
printed on recycled paper.[13]

Pencils can be made from 100 percent recycled paper. Greenciles, from http://greenciles.com, are one brand of pencils that your library can purchase and make available for your users, thus easily demonstrating your commitment to using recycled materials. Another environmentally friendly pencil is the rolled newspaper pencil. These pencils are made from whole newspaper sheets rolled around no. 2 pencil lead. They operate just like wood pencils, and users can actually read the newspaper lines from the pencil's original existence.

Close the Loop (www.closetheloop.com) is a Pennsylvania company that offers a wide variety of innovative recycled products and green building materials, including cardboard retractable pens made from recycled plastic collars, tips, and plungers and recycled cardboard. These pens can be customized with your library's logo, giving you another opportunity to sell recycled products.

Take a few minutes to count up the number of printers in your library. Multiply that by the number of times the toner cartridge needs to be replaced each year. The number you come up with represents a lot of potential waste that could take thousands of years to decompose in a landfill. Consider using an ink refill program rather than replacing the full cartridge. Ink refills are available to inject new ink into an existing printer cartridge, reducing your library's need to replace the actual printer cartridge. If you do not let the printer cartridge run out of ink before refilling it and use higher-quality paper (low-quality papers wear out the electric contacts on the print head faster), the printer cartridge may be refilled as many as eight times.[14] A variety of ink refill kits are available for every type of printer. To find the right kit for your printer, type in "ink refill kit" in any search engine and you will be connected to hundreds of product suppliers.

Notes

1. Definitions drawn in part from A. M. Gralton, What Is a Sustainable Product? (2009), www.altglobe.com/blog/what-sustainable-product.
2. For details, see www.conservatree.com/public/localsources/copypaper.html and www.conservatree.com/public/pubimages/readawrapper.gif.
3. See definitions and more at the Environmental Paper Network, www.environmentalpaper.org.
4. Stanford University, The 5R Recycling Program: Buying Recycled Paper, http://recycling.stanford.edu/5r/recycledpaper.html.

5. C. Memmott, New Chapter for Book Industry: "Green" Printing Methods, *USA Today*, www.usatoday.com/life/books/news/2005-08-01-green-publishing_x.htm.

6. Definitions from Conservatree, Environmental Definitions, www.conservatree.org/learn/Papermaking/Definitions.shtml, and Thomson-Shore, Recycled Paper Terms, www.thomsonshore.com/support_guidelines/glossary/recycled_paper_terms/.

7. Definitions from EcoLingo.com, Label Lingo, www.ecolingo.com/edu_LabelLingo.htm, and Forest Stewardship Council, Using the FSC Trademarks, www.fsc.org/17.html?&L=518%C3%9E%C2%88.

8. EcoLingo.com, Label Lingo.

9. Cornell University Library, Five Criteria for Evaluating Web Pages (1998), www.library.cornell.edu/olinuris/ref/research/webcrit.html.

10. U.S. Environmental Protection Agency, Recycling, www.epa.gov/epawaste/conserve/rrr/recycle.htm.

11. The following discussion of plastic types taken from IDES: The Plastics Web, Resin Identification Codes—Plastic Recycling Codes, www.ides.com/resources/plastic-recycling-codes.asp.

12. GreenerChoices.org, Toxics in Electronics, www.greenerchoices.org/electronicsrecycling/el_toxics.cfm.

13. For more discussion, see Conservatree, Recycled Paper: The Best Choice, www.conservatree.com/paper/PaperTypes/RecyBrochure.shtml.

14. PrintCountry, Printer Ink Cartridges Refill Kit Troubleshooting, www.printcountry.com/faq-troubleshooting-refill-kits.asp.

THE LIBRARY AS GREEN TEACHER

4

Programming is an essential part of a public library's community outreach and service. Each program a library creates and offers to its community should have a clearly defined set of goals and a plan for implementation, and it should provide attendees with the opportunity to learn through creative, thoughtful, and well-planned lessons, activities, or speeches. Programs are an excellent way to bring your community to your library and help its members go green.

Summer Reading Programs

Summer reading programs can interweave lessons on sustainability and environmental issues, making summer reading an opportunity to learn green ideas and develop green habits.

The Chicago Public Library embraced green summer reading in the summer of 2008, sponsoring its "Read Green, Live Green" program for children and adults (figure 4.1). The library's seventy-nine locations wove sustainability and environmental education throughout its summer reading activities and programs. The illustrated literature and reading program materials featured images of nature and our environment.

Squirrels, butterflies, flowers, and bees featured green tips on how an individual can make choices that help the environment. Environmental programs were included in the summer's activities, including interactive programs about garbage and environmental science and visits from authors who had written books about being green.

FIGURE 4.1
Chicago Public Library's 2008 "Read Green, Live Green" Program Image

Used with permission of the Chicago Public Library.

Chicago Public Library adult programs featured authors, politicians, and dancers sharing ideas about how the community could be environmentally aware. Here are a few examples:[1]

> **Green Parenting 101.** Join Manda Aufochs Gillespie, parent and author of "The Green Mama Blog," as she guides parents and caregivers through the various lifestyle options and consumer choices available for baby care, with an emphasis on reducing impact on the planet and on safeguarding baby's health. Find out more about Green Parenting 101 and the green mama at thegreenmama.com.
>
> **Vermicomposting for City Slickers.** Vermicomposting is the practice of using worms to turn organic food waste into a nutrient-rich soil instead of sending it to a landfill, where it can react to create greenhouse gases. In this hands-on workshop, learn the basics of this easy way to compost in an urban setting where outdoor compost bins may not be practical.

Summer reading at the Chicago Public Library in 2008 also included several innovative children's programs ranging from storytelling to arts and crafts, including these:

> **Marilyn Price: Recycle: Retell! The Story from Garbage.** Make a puppet using your imagination and some recycled objects and put them all together for a FUN-damental tale. This workshop will stretch your imagination and have you telling stories from easily made puppets. Boxes, soda bottles, milk cartons and an endless supply of everyday objects create the fun. All the workshops will end in a story told by the participants. Kids will also receive instructions and book lists.
>
> **Carol Lerner: Butterflies in the Garden. An Author Visit.** Join award-winning local author Carol Lerner as she discusses her nature books for children. Learn about butterflies and how to attract them and other pollinators to your own yard! Ms. Lerner will read from her book, *Butterflies in the Garden*.
>
> **Kidworks Touring Theatre Co.: Global Warming! What's a Kid to Do?** Journey with Kidworks in this educational and eye-opening performance. Kids of all ages can come ride a melting glacier with a penguin, journey to the Amazon

rainforest on a monkey, save the coral reef in Australia and help create a better future for our lives here in Chicago. Kidworks brings global warming myths and facts to life, and offers positive solutions to saving the air, the trees, the oceans and ourselves!

Steve Musgrave: Read Green, Live Green and Draw it All! Join renowned Chicago artist Steve Musgrave, creator of the artistic pieces of this and many past Summer Reading Programs at the Chicago Public Library, for a hands-on workshop to learn about nature drawing. Participants will learn how to create many of the shapes used in this year's Summer Reading Program artwork. Kids will also learn about artistic styles, techniques and materials.

The Chicago Public Library summer reading programs and activities each aimed to help the Chicago community learn about its role in environmental sustainability, while each participant worked his or her way through a personal summer reading adventure. The 2008 summer reading program is a great example of how a library can combine environmental leadership and environmental literacy with a public library's role in supporting reading, literacy, and personal growth.[2]

Even if you do not weave your entire summer reading program around green topics, you can encourage your community to visit the Environmental Defense Fund (EDF) and choose a title from "What Is the Most Influential Environmental Book?"[3] The EDF encourages public libraries to spread the word on their book lists and resources by offering a badge that can be placed on a library website. The EDF also sponsors a voting opportunity for readers to record their opinion of the book they feel has had the most influence on environmental learning. Your library could supplement the EDF program by displaying the books EDF has included on its list of most influential titles.

Other in-person programs can be restructured depending on your audience. Environmental lessons are often lessons that a whole family can learn together, and programs can be altered to reflect their audience.

Environmental Products Programs

Do you have a local hardware or grocery store in town? Consider inviting the store to collect and bring examples of products that could be used to make more environmentally friendly purchases. This could be a good opportunity for library patrons to learn about green products, as well as a great way for a local store to tell its community about the green products that are now available. For young adults, this program could focus on labels and how to know if a product is recycled or recyclable. Coloring sheets with what to look for when choosing products could be made available to children.

Green Fairs

Educate your community about green living and how to reduce its carbon footprint by sponsoring a green fair—a showcase of products, services, and resources that promote green initiatives and provide ideas on how individuals can live an ecologically smart lifestyle.

The Winter Park (Florida) Public Library partnered with its local Sierra Club office and the Central Florida Library Cooperative for a 2008 "Going Green Fair" that provided local businesses with the opportunity to sponsor the event and then showcase their product or service as a "Going Green" business. Sponsorships were available at different cost levels, and more than twenty-eight local businesses joined the fair. Business sponsors ranged from local appliance stores to larger retailers including Costco and Whole Foods. Doctors' offices and local car dealerships also joined in the fair.[4] A green fair can be a good way to raise the public's awareness of environmentally conscious consumer decisions, a good marketing campaign for the library, and a good fund-raising opportunity.

Another example of a green fair is the Altoona Area (Pennsylvania) Public Library's (www.altoonalibrary.org) "Keep Us Green and Growing Fair." This fair focused on presentations from area agencies on how Altoona residents could make small changes in their everyday lives that would help make the planet better. Examples of presentations included how to improve gas mileage and how to dispose of household trash.

Worm Farming Programs

The name may be enough to draw some people into the library. Worm farming is a way of turning vegetable and fruit scraps into a rich potting soil for a garden. Technically, a worm farm works by converting kitchen leftovers into worm fecal matter called worm casts. Worm casts can be added to garden soil to create a rich growing environment. Worm farms are an example of sustainable living practices. The Louisiana Department of Environmental Quality explains how:[5]

Goal

To teach attendees how to recycle food scraps into soil that can be used in their garden.

Materials

wood or plastic watertight container (the container should be about 12 inches long and at least 6 inches deep)
shredded newspaper
garden soil (about two handfuls per container)
crushed egg shells from cooked eggs (about two eggs per container)
about ten red worms (also called red wrigglers)
hand shovels
newspaper to protect tables and the floor

Instructions

Dampen the shredded newspaper. Place the damp newspaper, garden soil, and crushed egg shell in your container. Do not pack down this mixture. Add worms.
Add fruit and vegetable scraps to the worm farm. Also, starchy scraps such as bread, oatmeal, and pasta can be added. Red worms eat about half their body weight each day.

A worm farming program can be combined with information on worms and how they are an important contributor to our environment. One example of a fun website on worm education is The Adventures of Herman, which includes Herman (the worm's) autobiography in both English and Spanish.[6]

Rain Barrel Programs

Rain barrels are typically 55-gallon food-grade plastic barrels that can collect and store rainwater. Using rainwater for a garden allows a person to save money on water bills, keep storm water from flooding a foundation, and also take advantage of a renewable natural resource. Libraries can contact local recycling stores, food processing plants, or restaurants to obtain these barrels. Several preprogram steps are needed to prepare them for rain collection; note that some of these steps involve saws and other potentially dangerous tools and should be done by a knowledgeable craftsperson.[7]

Preprogram Steps

1. Clean out the barrel by scrubbing it with dish soap. Rinse the barrel with vinegar and water.
2. Cut a 6-inch-diameter hole in the lid of the barrel.
3. Cut and fasten a piece of window screen on the underside of the hole.
4. About 3 or 4 inches up from the bottom of the barrel, drill a hole that will accommodate a small faucet.

Goal

To teach attendees how rain can be saved and used in an individual's yard or garden.

Materials

Internet connection
speakers
projection screen
prewashed and prepared 55-gallon food-grade plastic barrel
brass faucet with 2- to 4-inch base
silicon caulk
paint, decorations, glue, and paint brushes

Instructions

Participants meet and learn about the effects of rainwater. Rainwater information, videos, and images are available at Rainwater Harvesting (http://rainwaterharvesting.tamu.edu).

After learning about rainwater, participants are matched with a rain barrel. Each participant uses the silicone caulk to attach the brass faucet toward the bottom of the rain barrel. Participants then decorate their rain barrels.

Participants in the rain barrel program follow these steps to set up their decorated rain barrel at home: Near the downspout of the home's existing rain gutter system, remove the elbow at the base of the downspout. The downspout may need to be shortened so that it ends just above the top of the rain barrel. Use the removed downspout elbow so that rainwater can be directed into the rain barrel's top hole. Once the rain barrel contains rainwater, attach a hose to the faucet to water the yard and garden.

Butterfly Garden Programs

Butterflies have important roles in our ecosystem: they pollinate fruits, flowers, and vegetables and provide food for other animals. Participants in your library's butterfly garden program can use the information they learn to build a garden that attracts butterflies.

Goal

To teach attendees how to attract butterflies to a garden, increasing local pollination of fruits, flowers, and vegetables.

Materials

> Internet connection
> speakers
> projection screen
> milkweed seeds

Instructions

> Search the Butterfly Website (http://butterflywebsite.com)
> database to discover which butterflies are in your state
> and choose a few videos to share with the group.[8]
> After showcasing local butterflies, highlight plants that are
> good for attracting butterflies to gardens, such as asters,

lavender, mints, purple coneflowers, thistle, and yarrow. Inviting a local gardener or a representative of a gardening club or garden store may also be a good idea.

Milkweed plants attract monarch butterflies. Milkweed seeds can grow almost anywhere in North America, and the seeds are available for free from Live Monarch Foundation. Write to Live Monarch—Seeds, 3003-C8 Yamato Road #1015, Boca Raton, FL 33434.

Your program can involve handing out milkweed seeds for participants to plant at home or having the group plant the seeds at the library. To plant the seeds at the library, you need potting soil, pots, and hand shovels for program participants.

The butterfly garden program can also include plans for building a butterfly house. Free butterfly house plans and instructions are available from the *Garden Gate* magazine website.[9] If some crafty library employees or volunteers are willing to create simple butterfly houses, a program on decorating a premade butterfly house could be a fun opportunity for your community to learn about the importance of butterflies within our ecosystem. Butterfly houses can be a great, colorful addition to a garden.

The public library can also set a community example by creating a butterfly garden on its grounds. The library grounds can also seek Wildlife certification through the National Wildlife Federation (NWF, www.nwf.org). Through the application process on the NWF website, the library documents the food and water sources in its garden, the places where young wildlife can be raised, and its sustainable gardening practices. Successful completion of the online application earns your library the Certified Wildlife Habitat designation. Seeking this honor can be a project taken on by the library staff, a Friends group, or a library teen organization.

One Book–One Community Programs

A one book–one community program focusing on sustainability can be directed to a family of readers and can help adults and young adults understand how human habits impact the environment. A book that brings sustainability directly down to the everyday choices that people make concerning how they dispose of their trash is Elizabeth Royte's

Garbage Land: On the Secret Trail of Trash. With this book the library can create a discussion via a blog or wiki.

Paul Fleischman's *Seedfolks* is another book that could be used in a one book–one community program. *Seedfolks* transforms a junk-strewn, rat-infested city lot into an urban oasis. This transformation changes the lives of the people who plant at the lot, developing a diverse new family. The vibrant characters from many different backgrounds help many different readers relate to the book, and the garden becomes a metaphor for the growth and changes of the human race.

Environmental Holidays Programs

There are many special days set aside each year to celebrate Earth. Your public library can plan special events for some or all of them:

February
    World Wetlands Day, February 2
March
    World Forestry Day, March 21
    World Water Day, March 22
    World Meteorological Day, March 23
    Earth Hour, toward the end of March each year
April
    World Health Day, April 7
    Earth Day, April 22
    National Arbor Day, the last Friday in April
May
    International Day for Biological Diversity, May 22
June
    World Environment Day, June 5
July
    World Population Day, July 11
August
    Smokey the Bear's Birthday, August 9
September
    National Wildlife Day, September 4

World Ozone Day, September 16
Green Consumer Day, September 28
October
World Animal Day, October 4
World Habitat Day, the first Monday in October
November
America Recycles Day, November 15

If you would like to group a series of activities into an annual week at your library, consider National Environmental Education Week (EE Week), which is held annually in April. Visit the National Environmental Education Foundation's website (www.eeweek.org) for more information on how to get involved in EE Week, links to teaching resources, and more information about the environment.

Online Programs

A library website is a powerful programming tool. Web-based library "programs," which are usually asynchronous, offer a library the ability to reach out to its community and provide learning opportunities to Internet users. Online library programs are well received when they offer interactive tools and games.

One fun tool that can be added to an online library program is the BP Energy Calculator from the Energy Lab at BP Global (www.bp.com).[10] In addition to the Energy Calculator, the Energy Lab guides users through energy's journey, offers an energy quiz, and provides energy facts. The Energy Calculator is particularly engaging. It helps users understand the components of their own carbon footprints and then provides a quantitative assessment of their individual impact on Earth. This tool, available in both Flash and non-Flash formats, asks users questions about their personal energy use, features of their home, how they dispose of trash, as well as the type of transportation they use. The report measures a person's carbon footprint in terms of CO_2 and provides suggestions on how to reduce that footprint. The BP Energy Calculator promotes self-reflection and is a good lead into a conversation about making better choices in our use of the environment.

Edenbee (http://edenbee.com) also measures a user's carbon footprint and then creates goals to help that individual or group reduce the footprint.

Users are able to develop their own carbon time line, and Edenbee sends e-mail reminders of steps to be taken to reduce the carbon footprint. A public library can create its own Edenbee profile and then share with its community how the library is effectively reducing its carbon footprint. Libraries may also want to point their users to My Emissions Exchange (www.myemissionsexchange.com), which pays individuals for reducing their home electricity usage.

EekoWorld (Environmental Education for Kids Online, http://pbskids .org/eekoworld/), conceived and developed by Bean Creative for PBS Kids Go and funded by the Corporation for Public Broadcasting's "Where Fun and Learning Click" initiative, is an interactive website geared toward elementary school children, who can create their own unique land-, air-, or water-dwelling EekoCreature and help it overcome environmental problems. An EekoHouse is also available for users to explore for conservation ideas. This interactive learning tool helps users understand the importance of their individual choices in taking care of Earth.

Video and sound are great additions to a web program. TeacherTube (www.teachertube.org) is an excellent source of videos about sustainability, conservation, and making the best personal choices for our environment. TeacherTube's goal is to provide an online community for sharing instructional teacher videos, lesson plan videos, and student works that are part of a lesson. Some unique titles in TeacherTube include "Water Conservation," "Did You Wonder," "Sustainability Footprints," and "Hate Something? Change Something!" TeacherTube is searchable by keyword and is an effective addition to an online library program.

Your library can also add original website content by creating pathfinders. Each pathfinder is a map of materials that match a specific interest. The appendix of this book provides three environmental pathfinders, featuring environmental books for children, young adults, and adults. You can use these pathfinders on your library's website to begin your community's green reading adventure.

Notes

1. Highlights contributed by Craig L. Davis, director of adult services of the Chicago Public Library.
2. More information on the Chicago Public Library 2008 "Read Green, Live Green" summer reading program is available at www.chipublib.org/dir_documents/SRP08

_Kidsa.pdf (children's program) and www.chipublib.org/dir_documents/srpa_08a .pdf (adult program).

3. Find the EDF list of influential books at www.edf.org/article.cfm?contentID=6470.

4. More information on the Winter Park "Going Green Fair" is available at www.cflc .net/goinggreenfair/.

5. Adapted from Louisiana Department of Environmental Quality, Making a Worm Farm (2008), www.deq.louisiana.gov/portal/tabid/2101/Default.aspx.

6. Herman's adventures are available at http://urbanext.illinois.edu/worms/.

7. There are many sites that explain this process. One of the best is www.epa.gov/ region3/p2/make-rainbarrel.pdf.

8. Find the database at http://butterflywebsite.com/articles/npwc/butterflychecklist .htm and the videos at http://butterflywebsite.com/shownaturevideos.cfm.

9. Find butterfly house plans and instructions at www.gardengatemagazine.com/ main/pdf/butterfly.pdf.

10. Go to the BP Energy Lab at www.bp.com/productlanding.do?categoryId=6941& contentId=7050870.

APPENDIX: Pathfinders

Environmental Books for Children
Created by Marisa Spooner Walstrum

Nonfiction

Callery, Sean. *I Wonder Why There's a Hole in the Sky and Other Questions about the Environment.* **New York: Kingfisher, 2008.**
This book, written by an elementary school teacher, discusses the questions of young readers about our environment, with answers written for ages 4–8. Chapters on weather, oil, and energy consumption cover a range of topics for young inquiring minds.

David, Laurie, and Cambria Gordon. *The Down-to-Earth Guide to Global Warming.* **New York: Orchard Books, 2007.**
This book explores answers to the questions children and adults face about global warming and its effects on our environment. Written for readers ages 7–12, it includes diagrams, illustrations, inspirational examples, and ideas for children's involvement in the fight against global warming. Author Laurie was the producer of the documentary film *An*

Inconvenient Truth; Gordon is a longtime children's author.
According to one recent review, "Children who take the book
to heart may start to help you in unexpected ways."

David, Sarah. ***Reducing Your Carbon Footprint at Home.*** **New York:
Rosen Central, 2009.**

This book is a collection of tips and ideas for children focused
on reducing their families' carbon footprints at home. Human
environmental impact is explained in scientific terms for
young readers. Illustrations, color photography, historical
information, and practical in-home projects make this a good
hands-on activity book and reference. Ages 7–12.

Ehlert, Lois. ***Waiting for Wings.*** **San Diego: Harcourt, 2001.**

The life cycle of a butterfly told in rhyme with colorful
illustrations is bound to increase your young reader's interest
in learning about how these creatures go from cocoon to
beautiful butterfly. Written for ages 3–7, this whimsical, easy
picture book contains recommendations on how to attract
butterflies to your garden.

Hewitt, Sally. ***Using Water.*** **New York: Crabtree, 2009.**

This book is a part of a "Green Team" series on environmental
issues for children ages 7–12. This volume is focused on
improving water conservation and the environment at the
local level to create a global impact. Published in the United
Kingdom, the series gives an international outlook on a global
problem. Simple action items and larger water conservation
projects for children are described.

Kalman, Bobbie. ***The Life Cycle of an Earthworm.*** **New York:
Crabtree, 2004.**

Exploring the life cycle of an earthworm from birth
to maturity through reproduction, this book explains
the importance of the earthworm to our environment.
Photographs and illustrations make this fact-filled book
accessible for readers ages 6–12.

Lerner, Carol. ***Butterflies in the Garden.*** **New York: HarperCollins, 2002.**

This factual book for children covers the life cycle of butterflies
and also gives ideas for how to attract them to your garden. The
foods they eat, the plants and flowers they use to lay eggs, and

their habitat are explained for readers ages 4–8. The beautiful full-page illustrations provide further engagement and excitement about attracting these winged creatures to the garden.

Reilly, Kathleen. *Planet Earth: 25 Environmental Projects You Can Build Yourself.* White River Junction, Vt.: Nomad Press, 2008. This collection of facts and trivia is also a great hands-on learning guide for children age 9 and older. The book presents environmental issues and solutions while offering activities that help children to learn about our planet's resources. Activities include building a worm composting castle, gardening projects, and wind-powered machines.

Fiction

Bethel, Ellie, and Alexandra Colombo. *Michael Recycle.* San Diego: Worthwhile Books, 2008. Join Michael, whose superhero power allows him to teach people about recycling. On this adventure, Michael cleans up a town and the people declare, "To Michael Recycle! The green-caped crusader, our super-green hero, the planet's new savior!" Ages 4–8.

Cherry, Lynne. *The Great Kapok Tree: A Tale of the Amazon Rain Forest.* San Diego: Harcourt, 2008. A tree and its inhabitants petition a man who is going to cut down the tree by whispering in his ear while he is dreaming, setting the tone for this mythical tale written for ages 4–8. The connection of this tree and the rainforest to the environment around it, and the larger global impact of forests, is the main theme of the story. The beautiful illustrations in this picture book inspire admiration in young readers.

Inches, Allison, and Pete Whitehead. *The Adventures of a Plastic Bottle: A Story about Recycling.* New York: Little Green Books, 2009. Readers learn about recycling from the perspective of a plastic bottle. Through diary entries, the plastic bottle takes us on a journey from the refinery plant, to the manufacturing line, to the store shelf, to a garbage can, and finally to a recycling plant where it emerges into its new life as a fleece jacket. Ages 4–8.

McMullan, Kate, and Jim McMullan. *I Stink!* **New York: Joanna Cotler Books, 2002.**

This tale of a New York garbage truck with attitude gives kids an idea of all the waste that is picked up by the trucks. With an A to Z approach to listing trash items, sound effects and larger-than-life illustrations of this truck come to life. An exciting tale of trash with a message for kids about where trash goes after the garbage can and the consequences of not cleaning it up. Ages 4–8.

Ward, Helen, and Wayne Anderson. *The Tin Forest.* **New York: Dutton Children's Books, 2001.**

This is a story of an old man living alone among garbage, cleaning it up in the daytime and dreaming of it at night. One day he is inspired to create a forest full of plants, animals, birds, flowers, and a kitty to keep him company out of the scraps of metal that surround him. This imaginative tale with detailed illustrations has the theme of hard work and creativity to inspire readers ages 4–10.

Wong, Janet, and David Roberts. *The Dumpster Diver.* **Cambridge, Mass: Candlewick Press, 2007.**

A tale of imaginative, resourceful children, this book encourages kids to think about how one man's trash is another's treasure. Steve and his friends dive into the dumpster in search of treasures, hose off their good finds, and think up creative uses for recycling the items. The fast-paced story includes quirky characters and offers detailed illustrations to engage young readers. Ages 3–7.

Marisa Spooner Walstrum is a graduate of Dominican University School of Library and Information Science and a librarian at National-Louis University in Chicago, Illinois. Walstrum teaches courses and workshops on digital information literacy and serves as a digital resource person for the university.

Environmental Books for Young Adults
Created by Larissa Garcia

Nonfiction

Gore, Albert. *An Inconvenient Truth: The Crisis of Global Warming.* **New York: Viking, 2007.**
This young-adult version of the award-winning documentary is shorter and easy to read but still retains the message of global warming, its effects, and the need for action. Young readers will immediately recognize the book's title, and the easy-to-grasp graphics and revealing before-and-after photos provide effective evidence of climate change. Age 12 and up.

Hoose, Phillip. *The Race to Save the Lord God Bird.* **New York: Farrar, Straus and Giroux, 2004.**
This thoroughly researched book reads like an adventure story and chronicles the extinction of the ivory-billed woodpecker in the United States, the first modern endangered species. Hoose weaves science, economics, and social and political history throughout the book and discusses what these encounters have taught us about preserving endangered animals. Ages 10–14.

MySpace Community, with Jeca Taudte. *MySpace/OurPlanet: Change Is Possible.* **New York: HarperCollins, 2008.**
Specifically for teens, this guide offers practical suggestions for being more eco-friendly. Common myths and important environmental facts are explored, and examples from MySpace peers and real-life stories from young environmentalists are sure to inspire the next generation. The book is printed on post-consumer recycled paper with vegetable oil–based inks. With a foreword by Tom Anderson, founder of MySpace. Age 12 and up.

Pringle, Laurence. *The Environmental Movement: From Its Roots to the Challenges of a New Century.* **New York: HarperCollins, 2000.**
A history of the environmental movement, this book introduces the key figures and important challenges facing the movement. Topics range from the establishment of national parks to the threat of global warming, with black-and-white photographs of both preservation and destruction. A comprehensive resource section is included. Ages 10–14.

Sivertsen, Linda, and Tosh Sivertsen. *Generation Green: The Ultimate Teen Guide to Living an Eco-Friendly Life.* **New York: Simon Pulse, 2008.**
This guide, geared specifically toward teens, provides an overview of important environmental issues and offers practical tips for green living, including how to shop, dress, eat, and travel. Suggestions for green college majors and careers are included. Interviews with environmental activist teens and celebrities provide additional inspiration for "Generation Green." Ages 10–17.

Sonneborn, Liz. *The Environmental Movement: Protecting Our Natural Resources.* **New York: Chelsea House, 2008.**
This history of the environmental movement describes the beginning of the movement, the efforts of early environmentalists in the United States, the heyday of the 1970s when the Environmental Protection Agency and landmark environmental legislation were established, and challenges to the movement in the 1980s and 1990s. The future of the movement is also explored, through the significant environmental issues of the twenty-first century. Ages 9–14.

Fiction

Cowan, Jennifer. *Earthgirl.* **Toronto: Groundwood Books, 2009.**
Written in blog format, this novel takes the form of an online confessional as 16-year-old Sabine Solomon is propelled into environmental activism after clashing with a driver over discarded McDonald's leftovers. Tensions rise as Sabine finds herself at odds with her meat-eating family and shopaholic friends. Although entertaining, this book also introduces young adults to environmental awareness through Sabine's own experiences. Age 12 and up.

Gauthier, Gail. *Saving the Planet and Stuff.* **New York: G. P. Putnam's Sons, 2003.**
When 16-year-old Michael loses his summer job, he agrees to work for family friends at an environmentalist magazine. He is humorously introduced to the 1960s-style environmentalism of Walt and Nora but soon finds he has a talent for the business as well as interesting summer vacation stories to tell

his friends. References to pop culture, mass consumerism, and environmental issues are included. Ages 9–12.

Hiaasen, Carl. *Hoot.* **New York: Alfred A. Knopf, 2002.**

Themes of environmental conservation and animal rights are explored as 13-year-old Roy is the new kid in a small Florida community who becomes involved in an attempt to save a colony of burrowing owls from a proposed construction site. This ecological mystery includes humor, charming characters, and touching scenes of children enjoying the wildness of nature. Ages 9–12.

———. *Flush.* **New York: Alfred A. Knopf, 2005.**

Hiaasen's second book for young adults focuses on the illegal dumping of raw sewage from a floating casino and again places an environmental issue in the hands of a kid. Noah Underwood's father has recently been jailed for sinking a riverboat, so it is up to Noah and his younger sister, Abbey, to gather evidence that the owner of the floating casino is emptying his bilge tanks into protected waters. Ages 9–12.

McNaughton, Janet. *The Secret under My Skin.* **New York: Eos/ HarperCollins, 2005.**

In the year 2368, humans exist under dire environmental conditions, and one young woman, rescued from a work camp and chosen for a special duty, uses her love of learning to discover the truth about the planet's future and her own dark past. This science fiction novel weaves environmental issues throughout the plot and also explores themes of education and science. Ages 12–16.

Nelson, Blake. *They Came from Below.* **New York: Tor Teen, 2007.**

Environmentalist themes are apparent throughout this science fiction novel as best friends Emily and Reese meet Steve and Dave while on summer vacation in Cape Cod. The two boys seem too good to be true, and their presence turns out to be related to a dire threat of global pollution. Age 12 and up.

Larissa Garcia is a graduate of Dominican University School of Library and Information Science and a librarian at National-Louis University in Lisle, Illinois. Garcia spearheads the LibGuides project at National-Louis, bringing together librarians and faculty from throughout the university to collaborate in the sharing of valuable online resources.

Environmental Books for Adults
Created by Don Pawl

Nonfiction

Blatt, Harvey. *America's Environmental Report Card: Are We Making the Grade?* **Cambridge, Mass.: MIT Press, 2005.**
> Somewhat surprisingly, Blatt, a geology professor, gives the United States A and A– grades for its handling of environmental issues related to air pollution and the ozone layer. Blatt offers some alternative ideas for energy savings and laments that the United States would serve itself better by limiting the rapid development of urban communities.

Buckingham, Susan, and Mike Turner, eds. *Understanding Environmental Issues.* **Thousand Oaks, Calif.: Sage, 2007.**
> Buckingham, Turner, and others have created an excellent informational resource targeted mainly at undergraduate students but specifically at those interested in geography, ecology, the environment, and the social sciences. The primary focus is for those interested in the teaching of environmental issues.

Dunaway, Finis. *Natural Visions: The Power of Images in American Environmental Reform.* **Chicago: University of Chicago Press, 2005.**
> *Natural Visions* is an interesting twist on environmental issues and how individuals might employ imagery as a source for conserving nature's treasured landmarks. Dunaway suggests that conservationists use photographs and coffee-table books of U.S. landmarks (e.g., Yellowstone) to promote an almost overzealous production of coffee-table books for political purposes.

McNeil, John Robert. *Something New under the Sun: An Environmental History of the Twentieth-Century World.* **New York: W. W. Norton, 2001.**
> McNeil explores the environmental deterioration of the world in the twentieth century in insightful but not overwhelming fashion. Because of the amount of damage human beings have inflicted on the earth, this book is not necessarily uplifting, but it is a valuable historical resource for explanations of the decline of the state of the environment.

Pahl, Greg. *The Citizen-Powered Energy Handbook: Community Solutions to a Global Crisis.* White River Junction, Vt.: Chelsea Green, 2007.

Pahl examines the energy challenges the citizens of the world face now and in the not-too-distant future. He provides encouraging accounts of communities working together to combat the reliance on hydrocarbon fuels in this must-read for citizens exploring alternative sources of energy.

Speth, James. *Red Sky at Morning: America and the Crisis of the Global Environment.* New Haven, Conn.: Yale University Press, 2007.

Speth takes aim at the United States for the proliferation of the current environmental challenges facing the world, despite some areas of improvement. He claims that bans on ozone-depleting chemicals have been helpful but believes countless conferences and other international agreements have done little to stem the degradation of the environment. Speth believes the United States is not looking hard enough for solutions to environmental challenges, which are only expanding as the population and technology continue to grow.

Fiction

Atwood, Margaret. *Oryx and Crake: A Novel.* New York: Nan A. Talese/Doubleday, 2003.

Atwood's novel paints an unsettling view of the future, with a young man trying to survive in a world ravaged by ecological disaster. The protagonist is faced with surviving in a world that has completely changed, and Atwood invites the reader to contemplate how dangerously close such an event could be.

Boyle, T. C. *A Friend of the Earth.* New York: Viking, 2000.

This engaging but grim tale is set in the year 2025, with protagonist Tyrone trying to survive in a world with rampant global warming—just as he had predicted some forty years earlier. Flashbacks throughout the novel reveal the many outlandish things Tyrone had done in his efforts to protect Earth, in turn causing him to lose his wife and spend time in jail. In what seems to be a theme in other works, Boyle suggests to the reader that the environmentalists can be just as troublesome with their efforts to protect the planet as those who have little regard for its well-being.

Grant, Richard. *Tex and Molly in the Afterlife*. New York: Avon Books, 1996

An older hippie couple die suddenly, and there is no peace and quiet for them in the afterlife. They end up fighting for an environmental cause (similar to when they were alive), but in the afterlife their fight involves several spiritual and comical encounters as they wage war against a company intent on destroying a forest and replacing it with plastic trees.

Hiaasen, Carl. *Sick Puppy: A Novel*. New York: Alfred A. Knopf, 1999.

A litterbug tosses a fast-food wrapper out the car window and so ensues a rather inventive and humorous tale of an individual frustrated with the lack of respect people have for the welfare of their planet. The protagonist decides to kidnap the dog of the litterbug to make him pay for his action but decides to take his wife as well and soon learns that the litterbug who first drew his ire is a political heavyweight with little regard for the natural lands of Florida—unless it involves making a buck.

Russell, Alan. *The Forest Prime Evil*. New York: Pocket Books, 1992.

A man dedicated to saving redwoods in California ends up dead and the mystery soon follows. Was he angering those who had little concern for the environment or the trees, or was he angering those who supported the conservation and safety of nature? A detective arrives on the scene to seek clues, but along the way he discovers some interesting similarities between those who support environmental conservation and those with less concern.

Siddons, Anne Rivers. *King's Oak: A Novel*. New York: Harper and Row, 1990.

Diana and her daughter flee from an abusive man and arrive in Georgia for a different kind of battle. Diana falls for a man who wants to protect the land he lives on at all costs. A nearby nuclear facility raises some questions about the safety of his land, and Diana joins him in the battle.

Don Pawl is a graduate of the University of Illinois School of Library and Information Science. Pawl currently works in the interlibrary loan department of Kraemer Family Library, University of Colorado, Colorado Springs.

RESOURCES

AgriLife Extension, Texas A&M System. Rainwater Harvesting.
    http://rainwaterharvesting.tamu.edu.

Alexander Street. Music Online. www.alexanderstreet.com/products/
    muso.htm.

Allen County Public Library, Genealogy Center. www.youtube.com/
    watch?v=tcqDqc0SXgo&feature=related.

Alliance for Biking and Walking. www.peoplepoweredmovement.org/site/.

Altoona Public Library. Keep Us Green and Growing Fair.
    www.altoonalibrary.org/v2scripts/comments.asp?blogid=45.

America Bikes. www.americabikes.org.

American Coatings Association. Glossary of Terms. www.paint.org/
    industry/glossary.cfm.

B Logistics. Marketplace Solutions. www.blogistics.com.

Bags on the Run. www.bagsontherun.com.

Baird, L., and the editors of *Yankee Magazine*. *Don't Throw It Out:
    Recycle, Renew, and Reuse to Make Things Last.* New York:
    Yankee Publishing, 2007.

Belcher, L. How to Choose a Low Flush Toilet. www.ehow.com/
    how_4493176_choose-low-flush-toilet.html.

Better World Books. www.betterworldbooks.com.

Big Sky Institute at Montana State University and the NBII Mountain Prairie Information Node. Butterflies of North America. http://butterflywebsite.com/articles/npwc/butterflychecklist.htm.

Book Crossing. www.bookcrossing.com.

Books for Soldiers. www.booksforsoldiers.com.

BP Energy Lab. www.bp.com/productlanding.do?categoryId=6941&contentId=7050870.

Brey-Casiano, C. A. "From Literate to Information Literate Communities through Advocacy." In *Current Practices in Public Libraries,* ed. W. Miller and R. M. Pellen, 181–190. Binghamton, N.Y.: Haworth Information Press, 2006.

Casabella. www.casabella.com.

Chicago Public Library. Read Green, Live Green Summer Reading Program. www.chipublib.org/dir_documents/SRP08_Kidsa .pdf.

———. Read Green, Live Green Summer Reads for Adults. www.chipublib.org/dir_documents/srpa_08a.pdf.

Cincinnati Public Library. Cincinnati Public Library Summer Reading Program 2009. www.youtube.com/watch?v=D_zD4uKVjBM.

Close the Loop, LLC. Recycled Retractable Pens. www.closetheloop .com/inforecycledpens.html.

Columbus Public Library. Discover a New World at Columbus Public Library. www.youtube.com/watch?v=s-oBHCsFbkk.

Conservatree. Copy Papers. www.conservatree.com/public/ localsources/copypaper.html.

———. Environment Definitions. www.conservatree.org/learn/ Papermaking/Definitions.shtml.

———. How to Read a Ream Wrapper. www.conservatree.com/public/ pubimages/readawrapper.gif.

———. Recycled Paper: The Best Choice. www.conservatree.com/ paper/PaperTypes/RecyBrochure.shtml.

Cornell University Library. Five Criteria for Evaluating Web Pages (1998). www.library.cornell.edu/olinuris/ref/research/webcrit .html.

Coyle, K. Environmental Literacy in America (2005). www.neefusa .org/pdf/ELR2005.pdf.

Delicious. http://delicious.com.

Earth 911. Making Every Day Earth Day. http://earth911.com.

Earthjustice. Global Warming. www.earthjustice.org/our_work/issues/
        global-warming/index.html.

Ecocycle. Alternative Cleaners and Recipes. www.ecocycle.org/
        hazwaste/recipes.cfm.

EcoLingo.com. Label Lingo. www.ecolingo.com/edu_LabelLingo.htm.

Ecollo. Searching for an Eco-Friendly Vacuum Cleaner (2008).
        www.ecollo.com/post/2008/10/Searching-for-an-Eco
        -Friendly-Vacuum-Cleaner.aspx.

Ecosilk Bags. www.bagladiesofseattle.com.

Edenbee. http://edenbee.com.

Environmental Defense Fund. What Is the Most Influential
        Environmental Book? www.edf.org/article.cfm?contentID=6470.

Environmental Leadership. Saving the Planet One Person at a Time.
        http://environmentalleadership.com/default.htm.

Environmental Paper Network. Paper Related Definitions.
        www.environmentalpaper.org/paper-definitions.html.

ERIC Development Team. "Environmental Literacy," ERIC/CSMEE
        Digest (ED351201 1992-11-00). www.eric.ed.gov/ERICDocs/
        data/ericdocs2sql/content_storage_01/0000019b/80/12/f4/a7.pdf.

Forest Stewardship Council. Using the FSC Trademarks. www.fsc
        .org/17.html?&L=518%C3%9E%C2%88.

Freecycle. www.freecycle.org.

Friends Book Sale. The Friends Book Sale Program. www
        .friendsbooksale.com/Program.htm.

Garden Gate. Butterfly House. www.gardengatemagazine.com/main/
        pdf/butterfly.pdf.

GardenFork. Viewer Forum. http://forum.gardenfork.tv.

———. Real World Green. "Visiting Your Public Library Makes You
        Green." www.gardenfork.tv/real-world-green/.

Goodman, J. Solar-Powered Landscape Lighting: The Alternative
        Energy Option. http://ezinearticles.com/?Solar
        -Powered-Landscape-Lighting,-the-Alternative-Energy
        -Option&id=970526.

Gorman, M. "The Value of Information for National Development."
        Keynote speech at Libraries: Networking for National

Development conference. Jamaica, November 22, 2007. www.nlj.gov.jm/NLJ/files/u1/Michael_Gorman.pdf.

Gralton, A. M. What Is a Sustainable Product? (2009). www.altglobe.com/blog/what-sustainable-product.

Green Forest. Introduction. www.greenforest-products.com.

Green Networld. Aluminum Recycling (1999). www.green-networld.com/tips/aluminium.htm.

Green Seal. About Green Seal. www.greenseal.org/about/index.cfm.

Greenciles. Environmentally Friendly Pencils. www.greenciles.com.

GreenerChoices.org. Products for a Better Planet. http://greenerchoices.org.

———, Electronics Reuse and Recycling Center. Toxics in Electronics. www.greenerchoices.org/electronicsrecycling/el_toxics.cfm.

Hands Across the Water. www.surplusbooksforcharity.org.

InspectAPedia. Electrical Definitions: Amps, Volts, Watts, Ground. www.inspect-ny.com/electric/ElectricalDefinitions.htm.

Integrated Design Engineering Systems (IDES). Resin Identification Codes—Plastic Recycling Codes. www.ides.com/resources/plastic-recycling-codes.asp.

International Society of Altered Book Artists. www.alteredbookartists.com.

Kansas State Department of Architectural Engineering and Construction Science. *GreenTech Bulletin* (2004). http://files.bnpmedia.com/EDC/Protected/Files/PDF/2005_01-GBTB-WaterlessUrinal.pdf.

Kessler, D. How to Shop Smart, Save Forests and Send a Message. www.treehugger.com/files/2009/02/greenpeace_how_to_shop_smart.php.

King County. Public Health—Seattle and King County. www.kingcounty.gov/healthservices/health/videos.aspx.

League of American Bicyclists. Features. www.bikeleague.org.

LibGuides. www.springshare.com/libguides/index.html.

Long, C. Energy Cost of PCs on Standby (2006). http://news.bbc.co.uk/1/hi/programmes/click_online/4929594.stm.

Louisiana Department of Environmental Quality. Making a Worm Farm (2008). www.deq.louisiana.gov/portal/tabid/2101/Default.aspx.

Marcal. Small Steps. www.marcalpaper.com.

McCook, K. *Introduction to Public Librarianship.* New York: Neal-Schuman, 2004.

Memmott, C. New Chapter for Book Industry: "Green" Printing
    Methods. www.usatoday.com/life/books/news/2005-08-01
    -green-publishing_x.htm.

Mikula, R. The Butterfly Website. http://butterflywebsite.com/
    shownaturevideos.cfm.

Mission Mop. Microfiber Mops: Why Ours Are Better.
    www.missionmop.org.

My Green Electronics. Enjoy Your Electronics: Protect the
    Environment. www.mygreenelectronics.org.

NASA. Safeguarding Our Atmosphere. www.nasa.gov/centers/glenn/
    about/fs10grc.html.

National Center for Biking and Walking. Bikewalk. www.bikewalk.org.

Natural Resource Defense Council. A Shopper's Guide to Home Tissue
    Products. www.nrdc.org/land/forests/gtissue.asp.

No Child Left Inside. Why Is Environmental Education Important?
    www.cbf.org/Page.aspx?pid=947.

Northwest Product Stewardship Council. What Is Product
    Stewardship? www.productstewardship.net/index.html.

NYC.gov. NYC Waste Le$$: Agencies and Schools. www.nyc.gov/html/
    nycwasteless/html/at_agencies/laws_directives.shtml.

Obama, B. "Bound to the Word." *American Libraries* (August 2005).
    www.ala.org/ala/alonline/resources/selectedarticles/obama05.cfm.

OCLC. ILLIAD—OCLC Resource Sharing and Delivery. www.oclc
    .org/illiad/.

Paper Recycles. Latest News. www.paperrecycles.org.

PBS Kids. EekoWorld (Environmental Education for Kids Online).
    http://pbskids.org/eekoworld/.

Penn State University Environmental Health and Safety. What Does
    an MSDS Tell You? www.ehs.psu.edu/help/info_sheets/msds
    _tips.pdf.

Printcountry.com. Printer Ink Cartridges Refill Kit Troubleshooting:
    Troubleshooting with Refill Kits. www.printcountry.com/faq
    -troubleshooting-refill-kits.asp.

Reach Out and Read National Center. How ROR Works.
    www.reachoutandread.org/about/.

Recipe Goldmine. Household Cleaning Recipes. www.recipegoldmine
    .com/house/house.html.

Recycling Centers. Find a Recycling Center in Your Area. www.recyclingcenters.org.

School and Community Assistance for Recycling and Composting Education. www.bookrescue.org.

Seventh Generation. www.seventhgeneration.com.

Society of the Plastics Industry. SPI Resin Identification Code—Guide to Correct Use. www.plasticsindustry.org/AboutPlastics/content.cfm?ItemNumber=823&navItemNumber=2144.

Stanford University. Buying Recycled Paper. http://recycling.stanford.edu/5r/recycledpaper.html.

Starfiber. The Original Starfiber. www.starfibers.com.

Supreme Court of the United States. Recent Decisions. www.supremecourtus.gov.

Teachers.net. Lesson Plans. http://teachers.net/lessons/.

Teacher Tube. www.teachertube.com.

Texas State Library and Archives Commission. CREW: A Weeding Manual for Modern Libraries (2008). www.tsl.state.tx.us/ld/pubs/crew/.

Thomson-Shore. Recycled Paper Terms. www.thomsonshore.com/support_guidelines/glossary/recycled_paper_terms.

United States Green Building Council. Welcome to USGBC. www.usgbc.org.

University of Akron, Department of Chemistry. The Chemical Database. http://ull.chemistry.uakron.edu/erd/.

U.S. Department of Transportation, Federal Highway Administration. Safe Routes to School. http://safety.fhwa.dot.gov/saferoutes/.

U.S. Environmental Protection Agency. Environmental Impact Statement (EIS) Database. www.epa.gov/compliance/nepa/eisdata.html.

———. Federal Insecticide, Fungicide, and Rodenticide Act (FIFA). www.epa.gov/agriculture/lfra.html#Summary%20of%20the%20Federal%20Insecticide,%20Fungicide,%20and%20Rodenticide%20Act.

———. Recycling. www.epa.gov/epawaste/conserve/rrr/recycle.htm.

———. RCRA Online. www.epa.gov/waste/inforesources/online/index.htm.

Virtual Museum of the City of San Francisco. Major Online Exhibits.
    www.sfmuseum.org.
Winter Park Public Library. Going Green Fair: Living a Sustainable
    Life. www.cflc.net/goinggreenfair/.

INDEX

You may also be interested in

Building Science 101: Designed for libraries where construction of a whole new building is not feasible, this book offers step-by-step instructions for improving the energy use of existing structures, with methods for being environmentally and fiscally responsible.

Small Business and the Public Library: Whether patrons need resources to start their own business, search for a new job, or locate demographic statistics to help them market their existing product, this resource will help you answer questions and meet their needs.

Designing Space for Children and Teens in Libraries and Public Places: Providing tips, suggestions, and guidelines on the critical issues that surround designing spaces for children and teens, this how-to book will help you create a space that they will never want to leave.

No Shelf Required: Editor Sue Polanka brings together a variety of professionals to share their expertise about e-books. Providing forward-thinking ideas while remaining grounded in practical information that can be implemented in all kinds of libraries, the topics explored include an introduction to e-books, e-book technology, and much more.

Order today at www.alastore.ala.org or 866-746-7252!
ALA Store purchases fund advocacy, awareness, and
accreditation programs for library professionals worldwide.